Xtreme Times
POWER

*Countering Antichrist
Spirit Forces*

KEITH W. FLETCHER

XTREME TIMES: Countering Antichrist Spirit Forces
Copyright © 2013 Keith W. Fletcher
ALL RIGHTS RESERVED

No part of this publication may be reproduced in any form without prior written permission.
Unless otherwise noted, all biblical references are quoted from the King James Version.

Produced by
KWF Ministries
www.keithfletcher.cc

All rights reserved.
ISBN: 1482653214
ISBN-13: 9781482653212

DEDICATION

Dedicated to everyone who is in the fight! This world is not our home; we're just passing through. While we are here, we're in a war, and from this war there is no discharge. Gird up, show up, fight the good fight, and understand that the battle is already won. We just have to exercise our authority!

CONTENTS

	Foreword	xi
1	Why Satan Hates You	1
2	Praying with Authority	7
3	Power in Pleading the Blood of Jesus	13
4	Binding and Loosing	17
5	Armor of God	21
6	Angels	35
7	Breaking Powers of Darkness	45
8	God	107
9	Baptism	117
10	Word Made Flesh	125
11	Holy Ghost Power!	131

ACKNOWLEDGMENTS

To my wife, Melissa: Thanks for putting into action in our home things in this book that make *the* difference! Thanks for allowing countless hours of work in the kingdom of God!

To my mother, Lena Fletcher, for exemplifying a prayerful life and a Christian walk in front of your children, grandchildren, and great-grandchildren that leaves no doubt of your love for God and family, and your compassion for humanity. Mother, I owe you a debt that I will never be able to scratch the surface of repaying.

Dad, Lonnie Fletcher, you're gone from this life, but more alive now than we who remain wrapped in these weak, cumbersome, flesh bodies. But one day, we'll see you on the other side! I'm doing my best to make it to see you.

To my son, Brayden; daughters, Toby and Courtney; and grandchildren, Marlie and Mason; there are gold nuggets in this book...they're found in the words of scripture organized among the pages of these writings.

To my sisters, Judy and Lynda, thanks for your unwavering support and prayer. Dale, I really appreciate all that you have done over the years.

Xtreme Times POWER

To mother-in-law, my brothers-in-law, and sisters-in-law, nieces, nephews you guys are the greatest! I love my family!

To my pastor, Rev. Jerry Dean, I do not have the vocabulary to form the thanks that I owe. I am forever grateful. Thanks for taking away the crutches.

FOREWORD

Nothing seems to create more curiosity in humanity than the ancient prophesies of God's Holy Word concerning the end of time. Evangelist Keith Fletcher has committed himself to search out these timeless truths in the Scriptures and put them into print in order for us to wade through these complicated subjects with more ease. The more we understand the signs of the times, the better prepared we can prepare for the rapture of the church. Paul said, in **1 Thessalonians 5:4** "But ye, brethren, are not in darkness, that that day should overtake you as a thief." If we truly wish to make certain that this day not catch us unawares it is incumbent that we all study to show ourselves approved. How easy it is for us to fall into lethargy and put afar off that great day of the Lord.

Writing this book was no small task. It has been my observation that the author is motivated purely by his desire to help prepare the church. He has traveled extensively across our nation to wake up sleeping saints and alert us all to the soon coming of the Lord.

As your enjoy this book allow these eternal truths to create in an expectancy in our spirits. The Lord is coming: And that, knowing the time, that now *it is* high time to awake out of sleep: for

Xtreme Times POWER

now *is* our salvation nearer than when we believed. The night is far spent, the day is at hand: let us therefore cast off the works of darkness, and let us put on the armour of light" (**Romans 13:11-12 (KJV)). This book will help you turn on the light.**

Rev. Jerry Dean
Pastor
Pentecostals of Bossier City

1

WHY SATAN HATES YOU

WHY SATAN HATES YOU

Why is satan so determined to eliminate the human race? Why does satan hate man so much that he takes joy in our suffering and death?

The answer is that satan hates God! God created man in His image. We are the sons of God, and one day we shall be like Him. We are the children of God and joint heirs with Christ.

Ephesians 1:14
14 Which is the earnest of our inheritance until the redemption of the purchased possession, unto the praise of his glory.

James 2:5
5 Hearken, my beloved brethren, Hath not God chosen the poor of this world rich in faith, and heirs of the kingdom which he hath promised to them that love him?

Revelation 21:7
7 He that overcometh shall inherit all things; and I will be his God, and he shall be my son.

Attributes of Lucifer, according to Ezekiel 28:
- *You were the seal of perfection, full of wisdom and perfect in beauty.*
- *You were in Eden, the garden of God; every precious stone was your covering.*
- *The workmanship of your timbrels and pipes was prepared for you on the day you were created…*
- *You were the anointed cherub who covers; I established you…*
- *Till iniquity was found in you…*
- *By the abundance of your trading, you became filled with violence within, and you sinned.*
- *Therefore, satan was cast out of heaven as a profane thing.*

Xtreme Times POWER

A number of Lucifer's attributes are listed here. He was created, which means that he did not exist before God created him. He did not exist before time, as God did. He was a guardian cherub (one of the highest forms of angels). The Hebrew word for "covers" in the phrase "cherub who covers" means protection or guard, so we can assume that Lucifer was a guardian angel.

What is satan's interest in you? Christians are people who do not accept the ways of this world. Satan is determined to turn individuals from God and to drag them back into the world from which they came. Why? Because if these individuals overcome satan and the world, they will receive eternal life. They will become kings and priests in God's kingdom, which is coming soon, and they will judge the angels. Yes, satan and his angels are very interested in you. They want a relationship with Christians, but this relationship is not an honorable one, nor is it one unto salvation for which they are looking. God gives grace, forgiveness, mercy, and life. Satan is not forgiving, nor is he merciful. He is a sadistic murderer!

Satan went from being the seal of perfection to a profane thing cast out of heaven. You, on the other hand, have the promise of eternal life and heaven that satan *once* had.

NEVER FORGET, the devil walks about like a roaring lion, seeking whom he may devour. Satan is a predator who will stalk his prey, waiting for an opportunity to strike and kill. It doesn't matter whether we are weak or strong in the faith. We are on his hit list, and he will do what it takes to bring us down. That is why we must be vigilant, always watching, and always praying that we do not become a victim of satan's devices.

WHY SATAN HATES YOU

THE WORD

Genesis 1:26
²⁶ And God said, Let us make man in our image, after our likeness: and let them have dominion over the fish of the sea, and over the fowl of the air, and over the cattle, and over all the earth, and over every creeping thing that creepeth upon the earth.

1 John 3:2
² Beloved, now are we the sons of God, and it doth not yet appear what we shall be: but we know that, when he shall appear, we shall be like him; for we shall see him as he is.

Romans 8:14-17
¹⁴ For as many as are led by the Spirit of God, they are the sons of God.
¹⁵ For ye have not received the spirit of bondage again to fear; but ye have received the Spirit of adoption, whereby we cry, Abba, Father.
¹⁶ The Spirit itself beareth witness with our spirit, that we are the children of God:
¹⁷ And if children, then heirs; heirs of God, and joint-heirs with Christ; if so be that we suffer with him, that we may be also glorified together.

Ezekiel 28:13-15
¹³ Thou hast been in Eden the garden of God; every precious stone was thy covering, the sardius, topaz, and the diamond, the beryl, the onyx, and the jasper, the sapphire, the emerald, and the carbuncle, and gold: the workmanship of thy tabrets and of thy pipes was prepared in thee in the day that thou wast created.
¹⁴ Thou art the anointed cherub that covereth; and I have set thee so: thou wast upon the holy mountain of God; thou hast walked up and down in the midst of the stones of fire.

Xtreme Times POWER

[15] Thou wast perfect in thy ways from the day that thou wast created, till iniquity was found in thee.

1 Peter 5:8
[8] Be sober, be vigilant; because your adversary the devil, as a roaring lion, walketh about, seeking whom he may devour:

2

PRAYING WITH AUTHORITY

PRAYING WITH AUTHORITY

God's mercies are new every day! When we pray, repenting—asking for clean hands and a clean heart—it is DONE. It is that fast. Then we may go on and pray with authority!

The devil would like to accuse us, to make us feel guilty, unworthy, not good enough, etc. These are all weapons of his. When we repent and pray for cleanliness, the righteousness of Christ gives us the promise and right to pray with authority.

The Bible doesn't tell us to live in fear of satan. *Be not afraid of their faces* is talking about demonic spirits. We have the power and authority to overcome evil through the righteousness of Jesus.

For I am with thee to deliver thee, we must believe and know He is with us to deliver us! *Behold, I have put my words in thy mouth.* Pray His Word! Pray His Word out loud. Praying His Word out loud builds your faith and binds evil spirits. The scriptural encouragements to "root out," "pull down to destroy," "throw down," and to "build" and to "plant" refer to the authority given to every saint of God to pull down satan's strongholds by praying with authority.

Pray out loud:

For the enemy to hear you. Pray the Word so that he will tremble and back off. Prayer is a weapon! **For us, faith cometh by hearing.** We only hear when we pray out loud!

How to maintain scriptural authority:
1. Separate yourselves unto God.
2. Put on the mind of Christ.
3. Believe.
4. Worship.
5. Abide in His Word.

Xtreme Times POWER

PRAYER MODEL

Lord, please forgive me for anything that I have participated in that was not of You. Cleanse and purify me, I pray. I ask You to cleanse my hands and cleanse my heart. I put on the armor of God, the mind of Christ, and I ask that You give me the heart of a servant. God, You gave us authority to trample satan under our feet. I take authority over evil and ask that You guide me and be a lamp unto my path.

From this point, pray the Word and bind and loose (see binding and loosing chapter 4) against current situations and circumstances, as needed.

COMPLETE PRAYER CLOCK
FINISH **START**

1. Praise
2. Praise
3. Forgiveness
4. Confession
5. Petition
6. Intercession
7. Read the Bible
8. Meditation
9. Thanksgiving
10. Pray the Word
11. Singing
12. Listening

COMPLETE PRAYER

PRAYER IS A WEAPON
Pray God's Word!

PRAYING WITH AUTHORITY

THE WORD

The Authority scripture

Jeremiah 1:7-10
⁷ But the LORD said unto me, Say not, I am a child: for thou shalt go to all that I shall send thee, and whatsoever I command thee thou shalt speak.
⁸ Be not afraid of their faces: for I am with thee to deliver thee, saith the LORD.
⁹ Then the LORD put forth his hand, and touched my mouth. And the LORD said unto me, Behold, I have put my words in thy mouth.
¹⁰ See, I have this day set thee over the nations and over the kingdoms, to root out, and to pull down, and to destroy, and to throw down, to build, and to plant.

2 Timothy 1:7
⁷ For God hath not given us the spirit of fear; but of power, and of love, and of a sound mind.

James 5:16
¹⁶ Confess your faults one to another, and pray one for another, that ye may be healed. The effectual fervent prayer of a righteous man availeth much.

2 Corinthians 6:17
¹⁷ Wherefore come out from among them, and be ye separate, saith the Lord, and touch not the unclean thing; and I will receive you.

Philippians 2:5
⁵ Let this mind be in you, which was also in Christ Jesus:

Xtreme Times POWER

1 Timothy 2:8
⁸ I will therefore that men pray everywhere, lifting up holy hands, without wrath and doubting.

John 4:23-24
²³ But the hour cometh, and now is, when the true worshippers shall worship the Father in spirit and in truth: for the Father seeketh such to worship him.
²⁴ God is a Spirit: and they that worship him must worship him in spirit and in truth.

John 14:12-14
¹² Verily, verily, I say unto you, He that believeth on me, the works that I do shall he do also; and greater works than these shall he do; because I go unto my Father.
¹³ And whatsoever ye shall ask in my name, that will I do, that the Father may be glorified in the Son.
¹⁴ If ye shall ask any thing in my name, I will do it.

John 15:7
⁷ If ye abide in me, and my words abide in you, ye shall ask what ye will, and it shall be done unto you.

3

POWER IN PLEADING THE BLOOD OF JESUS

POWER IN PLEADING THE BLOOD OF JESUS

PLEAD THE BLOOD OF JESUS!
CLAIM THE BLOOD OF JESUS!

PLEAD THE BLOOD OF JESUS! Pleading the blood of Jesus Christ simply means applying the blood to our life and circumstances just like the Israelites applied it to their door posts and were protected from the destroyer (Exodus 12).

Pleading the blood of Jesus is taking authority and power available to us by the death and resurrection of Jesus.

Plead the blood of Jesus over:
- Today
- My family
- Church family
- The nation, state, and city

The blood of Jesus is our only counteragent. When there is no blood covering, sin is free to corrupt and destroy.

PRAYER MODEL

Lord, I plead the blood over this day, over my time with You and keep this conversation private from the enemy.

CLAIM THE BLOOD OF JESUS (as it applies to your life).

PRAYER MODEL

I continue to trust Your mercy. Hide me in Your blood and keep me from unrighteousness. Forgive my presumptuous sins, my

wickedness (my desires to sometimes step outside the laws of God), and my iniquities. Search me and cleanse me.

THE WORD

Exodus 12:13
¹³ And the blood shall be to you for a token upon the houses where ye are: and when I see the blood, I will pass over you, and the plague shall not be upon you to destroy you, when I smite the land of Egypt.

Leviticus 8:30
³⁰ And Moses took of the anointing oil, and of the blood which was upon the altar, and sprinkled it upon Aaron, and upon his garments, and upon his sons, and upon his sons' garments with him; and sanctified Aaron.

Revelation 12:11
¹¹ And they overcame him by the blood of the Lamb, and by the word of their testimony; and they loved not their lives unto the death.

Psalm 19:13-14
¹³ Keep back thy servant also from presumptuous sins; let them not have dominion over me: then shall I be upright, and I shall be innocent from the great transgression.
¹⁴ Let the words of my mouth, and the meditation of my heart, be acceptable in thy sight, O LORD, my strength, and my redeemer.

4

BINDING AND LOOSING

TEARING DOWN STRONGHOLDS

BINDING AND LOOSING

TEARING DOWN STRONGHOLDS

BINDING AND LOOSING

BINDING AND LOOSING

The *tongue* is powerful! Be careful how you use it.

BINDING: *Forbidding, prohibiting*
LOOSING: *Permitting*

In Matthew 18:18, Jesus gave Peter "the keys of the kingdom of heaven" and told him "whatever you bind on earth will be bound [literally, "shall have been bound"] in heaven, and whatever you loose on earth will be loosed ["shall have been loosed"] in heaven." This means that Peter was granted the authority to pronounce the freedom or condemnation of a person, based on that person's response to the gospel. The verb tense "shall have been" indicates that this fact was already established in the will of the Father.

In Matthew 18:18, Jesus spoke the same words to all of the disciples, granting them authority in matters of church discipline.

We have been given the authority to bind and loose and the promise that it shall be done.

BINDING: *Forbidding, prohibiting*
LOOSING: *Permitting*

TEARING DOWN STRONGHOLDS

It's not our battle; it's God's!
We have to **choose** the power in our lives. Cast down all arguments! Bring every thought into captivity!

Xtreme Times POWER

Exodus 34:12
¹² Take heed to thyself, lest thou make a covenant with the inhabitants of the land whither thou goest, lest it be for a snare in the midst of thee:

PRAYER MODEL

Jesus, I refuse to let satan build strongholds against the kingdom of God and the plan of God. In the name of Jesus, I pull down the strongholds of darkness influencing our communities and nation. I cast down the vain imaginations that satan is using to dominate the philosophies affecting our culture, our world, and our homes. Lord, do not allow my mind to be filled with such hopelessness that I will accept an unchangeable situation that I know is against the purpose of God. In the name of Jesus.

THE WORD

Exodus 12:13
¹³ And the blood shall be to you for a token upon the houses where ye are: and when I see the blood, I will pass over you, and the plague shall not be upon you to destroy you, when I smite the land of Egypt.

Leviticus 8:30
³⁰ And Moses took of the anointing oil, and of the blood which was upon the altar, and sprinkled it upon Aaron, and upon his garments, and upon his sons, and upon his sons' garments with him; and sanctified Aaron.

5

ARMOR OF GOD

Ephesians 6:13-18

ARMOR OF GOD

Ephesians 6:13-18

¹³ Wherefore take unto you the whole armour of God, that ye may be able to withstand in the evil day, and having done all, to stand.

¹⁴ Stand therefore, having your loins girt about with truth, and having on the breastplate of righteousness;

¹⁵ And your feet shod with the preparation of the gospel of peace;

¹⁶ Above all, taking the shield of faith, wherewith ye shall be able to quench all the fiery darts of the wicked.

¹⁷ And take the helmet of salvation, and the sword of the Spirit, which is the word of God:

¹⁸ Praying always with all prayer and supplication in the Spirit, and watching thereunto with all perseverance and supplication for all saints.

HELMET OF SALVATION

Protect my mind, eyes and ears!

The helmet protects the head or the mind. It also protects the eyes and the ears.

PRAYER MODEL

Keep my mind from thinking evil. Protect my ears from hearing ungodly things, and keep my eyes from watching, reading, or seeing anything evil. Keep my eyes focused on You! Let me think right; let me see through eyes of the spirit—through Your eyes, God. I ask that You create in me a clean heart and renew within me a right spirit.

Xtreme Times POWER

THE WORD

Psalm 101:3
³ I will set no wicked thing before mine eyes: I hate the work of them that turn aside; it shall not cleave to me.

Romans 8:6-8
⁶ For to be carnally minded is death; but to be spiritually minded is life and peace.
⁷ Because the carnal mind is enmity against God: for it is not subject to the law of God, neither indeed can be.
⁸ So then they that are in the flesh cannot please God.

BREASTPLATE OF RIGHTEOUSNESS

Keep my heart right!

The breastplate of righteousness protects the vital organs. It protects the heart!

PRAYER MODEL

God, filter everything that comes into or out of my heart through Your righteousness. None is righteous, Lord, but You. Let me be easily impressed by Your spirit, recognizing the unction of Your spirit.

THE WORD

Ephesians 4:22-32
²² That ye put off concerning the former conversation the old man, which is corrupt according to the deceitful lusts;

ARMOR OF GOD

²³ And be renewed in the spirit of your mind;
²⁴ And that ye put on the new man, which after God is created in righteousness and true holiness.
²⁵ Wherefore putting away lying, speak every man truth with his neighbour: for we are members one of another.
²⁶ Be ye angry, and sin not: let not the sun go down upon your wrath:
²⁷ Neither give place to the devil.
²⁸ Let him that stole steal no more: but rather let him labour, working with his hands the thing which is good, that he may have to give to him that needeth.
²⁹ Let no corrupt communication proceed out of your mouth, but that which is good to the use of edifying, that it may minister grace unto the hearers.
³⁰ And grieve not the holy Spirit of God, whereby ye are sealed unto the day of redemption.
³¹ Let all bitterness, and wrath, and anger, and clamour, and evil speaking, be put away from you, with all malice:
³² And be ye kind one to another, tenderhearted, forgiving one another, even as God for Christ's sake hath forgiven you.

Psalm 23:3
³ He restoreth my soul: he leadeth me in the paths of righteousness for his name's sake.

Hosea 10:12
¹² Sow to yourselves in righteousness, reap in mercy; break up your fallow ground: for it is time to seek the LORD, till he come and rain righteousness upon you.

Xtreme Times POWER

Hebrews 10:22-23

²² Let us draw near with a true heart in full assurance of faith, having our hearts sprinkled from an evil conscience, and our bodies washed with pure water.
²³ Let us hold fast the profession of our faith without wavering; (for he is faithful that promised).

Ephesians 5:3-5

³ But fornication, and all uncleanness, or covetousness, let it not be once named among you, as becometh saints;
⁴ Neither filthiness, nor foolish talking, nor jesting, which are not convenient: but rather giving of thanks.
⁵ For this ye know, that no whoremonger, nor unclean person, nor covetous man, who is an idolater, hath any inheritance in the kingdom of Christ and of God.

BELT OF TRUTH

Protect me with truth, wrap Yourself around me, keep me from lies and error!

Proverbs 6:16-19

¹⁶ These six things doth the LORD hate: yea, seven are an abomination unto him:
¹⁷ A proud look, a lying tongue, and hands that shed innocent blood,
¹⁸ A heart that deviseth wicked imaginations, feet that be swift in running to mischief,
¹⁹ A false witness that speaketh lies, and he that soweth discord among brethren.

The Lord hates:
- Haughty: overly proud, snobbish, conceited, stuck-up, snooty

ARMOR OF GOD

- Dissension: problems, strife (making trouble)
- Lying tongue: stretching the truth, telling only part of the truth, or misrepresentationInnocent blood-shedding: backbiting, gossip, talking about family, friends, and church familyA wicked heart: evil, sinful, bad, gross, satanic, immoral, making trouble
- Feet quick to rush to evil: always doing things that are sinful
- False witness: gossiping, lying
- Premeditated: deliberate, planned, prearranged, willful

PRAYER MODEL

God, help me not to sin. I never want to push You so far that when I really need You, You aren't there because I took advantage of You and what You have done for me.

Advocate. Plead the cause for me; stand up for me; support me.

Jesus, help me to always honor Your words of truth and remind me that I do have a chance as long as I try to do my best for You. Thank You for giving me another chance to do right. In the name of Jesus.

Help me, God, not to be unkind to anyone, even those who don't like me. Help me to love them anyway. I don't want to disobey Your Word. I love and respect You, Father, and I give thanks for everything that You have done for me.

God, help me never to think of myself more highly than I think of anyone else. I am who I am through You and I want to be just like You, and think and act like You, too.

Xtreme Times POWER

Jesus, help me to know that the Word of God is truth. Everything written in Your Word is what You want for and expect of me. Help me to know that sin only lasts for a little while. Help me not to sin, because when I do, I sin against You. Help me to trust You, even when the way is unclear. I know that You hear every prayer that I pray.

THE WORD

Hebrews 11:25
^{25} Choosing rather to suffer affliction with the people of God, than to enjoy the pleasures of sin for a season.

2 Corinthians 5:7
^{7} For we walk by faith, not by sight.

Ephesians 6:14
^{14} Stand therefore, having your loins girt about with truth, and having on the breastplate of righteousness;

Hebrews 10:26
^{26} For if we sin willfully after that we have received the knowledge of the truth, there remaineth no more sacrifice for sins.

1 John 2:1
^{1} My little children, these things write I unto you, that ye sin not. And if any man sin, we have an advocate with the Father, Jesus Christ the righteous:

Philippians 2:2-5
^{2} Fulfill ye my joy, that ye be likeminded, having the same love, being of one accord, of one mind.

ARMOR OF GOD

³ Let nothing be done through strife or vainglory; but in lowliness of mind let each esteem other better than themselves.
⁴ Look not every man on his own things, but every man also on the things of others.
⁵ Let this mind be in you, which was also in Christ Jesus.

Colossians 3:12-15
¹² Put on therefore, as the elect of God, holy and beloved, bowels of mercies, kindness, humbleness of mind, meekness, longsuffering;
¹³ Forbearing one another, and forgiving one another, if any man have a quarrel against any: even as Christ forgave you, so also do ye.
¹⁴ And above all these things put on charity, which is the bond of perfectness.
¹⁵ And let the peace of God rule in your hearts, to the which also ye are called in one body; and be ye thankful.

Hebrews 6:18
¹⁸ That by two immutable things, in which it was impossible for God to lie, we might have a strong consolation, who have fled for refuge to lay hold upon the hope set before us:

SHOES OF PEACE

Be ready for combat, shod with the gospel of peace!

Be not easily provoked, nor prone to quarrel; but show all gentleness and all long-suffering to all men.

Ephesians 4:26
²⁶ Be ye angry, and sin not: let not the sun go down upon your wrath:

Xtreme Times POWER

PRAYER MODEL

God, guide my feet and protect them. Set my feet on firm ground, safe from the enemy. Everywhere I walk, help me to be a peacemaker. Send angels to make the rough places smooth so that I don't bruise my feet.

THE WORD

Isaiah 52:7
[7] How beautiful upon the mountains are the feet of him that bringeth good tidings, that publisheth peace; that bringeth good tidings of good, that publisheth salvation; that saith unto Zion, Thy God reigneth!

Romans 5:1-2
[1] Therefore being justified by faith, we have peace with God through our Lord Jesus Christ:
[2] By whom also we have access by faith into this grace wherein we stand, and rejoice in hope of the glory of God.

SHIELD OF FAITH

Faith must be our shield.

Faith is confidence in a person or thing; belief in God.

Consider faith to be the evidence of things not seen and the substance of things hoped for. Having faith—receiving Christ and the benefits of redemption, and so deriving grace from Him—is like a shield, a universal defense.

ARMOR OF GOD

Just as Jesus had faith enough to believe that we were worth dying for, so should we have faith in Him, whose shed blood has the power to save us from the penalty of sin.

PRAYER MODEL

God, You are the author and finisher of my faith. I receive my faith from You, because You are faithful. Destroy all of the fiery darts of the enemy and help me to understand. I pray for wisdom to understand that sin destroys faith. Give me a desire to study Your Word so that I won't sin against You. Help me to remember to praise seven times a day so that my faith is strengthened in You. Correct me when I do wrong and help me to learn from my mistakes. Help me to understand Your love for me.

THE WORD

Ephesians 6:16
16 Above all, taking the shield of faith, wherewith ye shall be able to quench all the fiery darts of the wicked.

Hebrews 11:1
1 Now faith is the substance of things hoped for, the evidence of things not seen

Proverbs 3:5-7
5 Trust in the LORD with all thine heart; and lean not unto thine own understanding.
6 In all thy ways acknowledge him, and he shall direct thy paths.
7 Be not wise in thine own eyes: fear the LORD, and depart from evil.

Xtreme Times POWER

Proverbs 18:10
¹⁰ The name of the LORD is a strong tower: the righteous runneth into it, and is safe.

Romans 8:31
³¹ What shall we then say to these things? If God be for us, who can be against us?

Philippians 4:6-7
⁶ Be careful for nothing; but in every thing by prayer and supplication with thanksgiving let your requests be made known unto God.
⁷ And the peace of God, which passeth all understanding, shall keep your hearts and minds through Christ Jesus.

SWORD OF THE SPIRIT

It is called the sword of the spirit the spirit indicts, and He renders it effective, powerful, and sharper than a two-edged sword.

We should mean what we say. Feigned prayers are fruitless; but if our hearts lead our prayers, God will meet them with his favor. Let the high praises of God be in our mouths!

And He hath made my mouth powerfully eloquent by the utterance of words which would penetrate the heart like a sharp sword.

Man needs bread, but bread is not all he needs. Material gratification of the appetites can never satisfy the deepest longings of the human spirit. The Word of God renews and replenishes the spirit.

ARMOR OF GOD

Let God put His words in our mouths rather than the eloquent, fleshly, flowery conversation of an empty man's wisdom. When it is the power of God, eloquence is immaterial and God is glorified instead of man. God is able to operate with His Word, judging and dividing asunder soul and spirit.

PRAYER MODEL

God, help me to understand that Your Word divides good from bad. Your Word judges my soul and thoughts to help me realize what is pure and what is evil. God, I believe, but help my unbelief that I can be more like You. Help me to realize that wherever I go and whatever I do, You see me. You know my thoughts and my heart. I ask, God, that You create within me a pure heart and a pure mind covered by Your blood. I ask that You put Your words in my mouth; that my speech be directed by Your spirit to Your glory. I plead the blood over all of my thoughts, my mind, and all that I do, that it would please and glorify You!

THE WORD

Ephesians 6:17
17 And take the helmet of salvation, and the sword of the Spirit, which is the word of God:

Psalm 17:4
4 Concerning the works of men, by the word of thy lips I have kept me from the paths of the destroyer.

Psalm 149:6
6 Let the high praises of God be in their mouth, and a two-edged sword in their hand.

Xtreme Times POWER

Isaiah 49:2
² And he hath made my mouth like a sharp sword; in the shadow of his hand hath he hid me, and made me a polished shaft; in his quiver hath he hid me.

Luke 4:4
⁴ And Jesus answered him, saying, It is written, That man shall not live by bread alone, but by every word of God.

1 Corinthians 2:4-5
⁴ And my speech and my preaching was not with enticing words of man's wisdom, but in demonstration of the Spirit and of power:
⁵ That your faith should not stand in the wisdom of men, but in the power of God.

Hebrews 4:12
¹² For the word of God is quick, and powerful, and sharper than any two-edged sword, piercing even to the dividing asunder of soul and spirit, and of the joints and marrow, and is a discerner of the thoughts and intents of the heart.

Hebrews 11:16
¹⁶ But now they desire a better country, that is, an heavenly: wherefore God is not ashamed to be called their God: for he hath prepared for them a city.

6

ANGELS

ANGELS

We do not pray to angels. We pray only to God! Angels are messengers of God. God dispatches angels on our behalf.

Revelation 22:8-9
8 And I John saw these things, and heard them. And when I had heard and seen, I fell down to worship before the feet of the angel which shewed me these things.
9 Then saith he unto me, See thou do it not: for I am thy fellowservant, and of thy brethren the prophets, and of them which keep the sayings of this book: worship God.

ANGELS

Seven divisions of angels exist.
1. Mighty angels
2. Guardian angels
3. Ministering angels
4. Elect angels
5. Archangels
6. Cherubim angels
7. Seraphim angels

THE WORD

2 Corinthians 10:4
4 (For the weapons of our warfare are not carnal, but mighty through God to the pulling down of strong holds;)

2 Peter 2:11
11 Whereas angels, which are greater in power and might, bring not railing accusation against them before the Lord.

Xtreme Times POWER

MIGHTY ANGELS

Mighty angels are heaven's warriors. They fight for the things of God!

PRAYER MODEL

I bind Satan in my city.
I come against evil and destroy it in my city.
Let the economy flourish.
Make it easy to do right in my city.
Make it easy to get saved.
Post an angel on the corners of my city.

THE WORD

Psalm 103:20
[20] Bless the LORD, ye his angels, that excel in strength, that do his commandments, hearkening unto the voice of his word.

Revelation 10:1-3
[1] And I saw another mighty angel come down from heaven, clothed with a cloud: and a rainbow was upon his head, and his face was as it were the sun, and his feet as pillars of fire:
[2] And he had in his hand a little book open: and he set his right foot upon the sea, and his left foot on the earth,
[3] And cried with a loud voice, as when a lion roareth: and when he had cried, seven thunders uttered their voices.

GUARDIAN ANGELS

Guardian angels are sent from God to protect!

ANGELS

Your prayers work for others!

PRAYER MODEL

Pray that God will send guardian angels to new converts to protect and guide them; to children; to elderly saints in the church; and to the children of ministers, missionaries, pastors, and evangelists.

THE WORD

Matthew 18:10
10 Take heed that ye despise not one of these little ones; for I say unto you, That in heaven their angels do always behold the face of my Father which is in heaven.

Exodus 23:20
20 Behold, I send an Angel before thee, to keep thee in the way, and to bring thee into the place which I have prepared.

Psalm 34:7
7 The angel of the LORD encampeth round about them that fear him, and delivereth them.

Hebrews 1:13-14
13 But to which of the angels said he at any time, Sit on my right hand, until I make thine enemies thy footstool?
14 Are they not all ministering spirits, sent forth to minister for them who shall be heirs of salvation?

Xtreme Times POWER

MINISTERING ANGELS

Ministering angels minister to *our* needs.

PRAYER MODEL

**Pray that God will send ministering angels to:
The sick, to encourage them and lift them up;
Saints, to minister to their spiritual needs;
Saints, to minister to their financial needs;
Recovering addicts, to encourage them and support them against discouragement;
Missionaries, to minister to them and encourage them.**

THE WORD

Hebrews 1:14
[14] Are they not all ministering spirits, sent forth to minister for them who shall be heirs of salvation?

Acts 27:23
[23] For there stood by me this night the angel of God, whose I am, and whom I serve.

ELECT ANGELS

Elect angels minister to the needs of the church.

PRAYER MODEL

Pray that God will send elect angels for the souls of everyone in your congregation. Pray that saints will pay their tithes and

ANGELS

offerings as the Word of God instructs us to do. Pray that the saints of God will be a positive influence on everyone who attends service or participates in any activities of the church body.

THE WORD

Acts 12:11
¹¹ And when Peter was come to himself, he said, Now I know of a surety, that the Lord hath sent his angel, and hath delivered me out of the hand of Herod, and from all the expectation of the people of the Jews.

ARCHANGELS

Archangels are friends to the saints of God, followers of Christ.

PRAYER MODEL

Pray that God will send archangels:
The archangel will stand up and deliver us in the time of trouble.

THE WORD

Daniel 12:1
¹ And at that time shall Michael stand up, the great prince which standeth for the children of thy people: and there shall be a time of trouble, such as never was since there was a nation even to that same time: and at that time thy people shall be delivered, every one that shall be found written in the book.

CHERUBIM

Cherubim's are protectors in various instances of God's holiness on the earth.

PRAYER MODEL

Pray that God will send Cherubims to protect all things pertaining to the holiness of God.

THE WORD

Hebrews 9:5
⁵ And over it the cherubims of glory shadowing the mercyseat; of which we cannot now speak particularly.

SERAPHIM

Seraphim angels are in charge of:
- Salvation
- Restoring God's people and His purpose for their lives
- Reviving God's people and His purpose for their lives
- Revival

PRAYER MODEL

Pray that God will send seraphim angels to save, restore, and revive those who need it. (Speak those individuals' names.)

ANGELS

THE WORD

Revelation 22:16
¹⁶ I Jesus have sent mine angel to testify unto you these things in the churches. I am the root and the offspring of David, and the bright and morning star.

Isaiah 6:6
⁶ Then flew one of the seraphims unto me, having a live coal in his hand, which he had taken with the tongs from off the altar:

7

BREAKING POWERS OF DARKNESS

2 Corinthians 10:3-4
³ For though we walk in the flesh, we do not war after the flesh:
⁴ (For the weapons of our warfare are not carnal, but mighty through God to the pulling down of strong holds.)

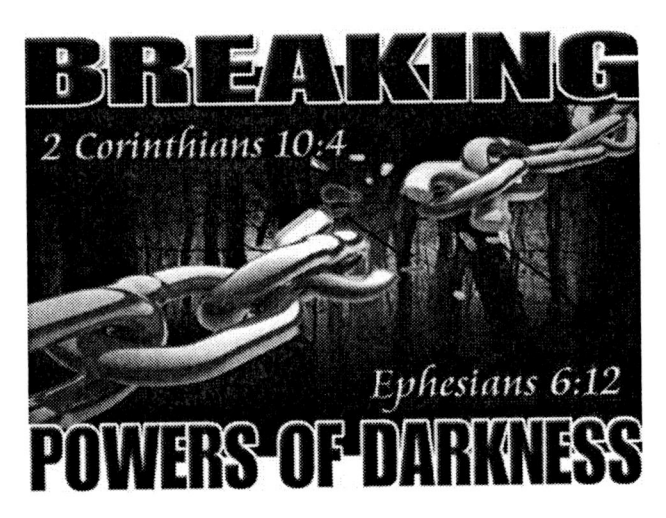

Ephesians 6:12
¹² For we wrestle not against flesh and blood, but against principalities, against powers, against the rulers of the darkness of this world, against spiritual wickedness in high places.

BREAKING POWERS OF DARKNESS

Matthew 12:29
²⁹ Or else how can one enter into a strong man's house, and spoil his goods, except he first bind the strong man? and then he will spoil his house.

SPIRIT OF DIVINATION

Spirit of divination is the practice of attempting to foretell future events or discern hidden knowledge by supernatural means.

God's Word shows that God's prophets receive their divine revelations by the Holy Ghost. On the other side of the spectrum are demonic spirits that feed information to fortune-tellers and sorcerers.

God's word also reveals that God wants to work through his children against the power of evil.

The battle of the universe is satan against God, and we must choose which side we prefer. There is no middle ground.

BIND the Spirit of Divination

Matthew 18:18
¹⁸ Verily I say unto you, Whatsoever ye shall bind on earth shall be bound in heaven: and whatsoever ye shall loose on earth shall be loosed in heaven.

LOOSE the Holy Spirit; Gifts of the Spirit

1 Corinthians 12:9-12
⁹ To another faith by the same Spirit; to another the gifts of healing by the same Spirit;

Xtreme Times POWER

[10] To another the working of miracles; to another prophecy; to another discerning of spirits; to another divers kinds of tongues; to another the interpretation of tongues:
[11] But all these worketh that one and the selfsame Spirit, dividing to every man severally as he will.
[12] For as the body is one, and hath many members, and all the members of that one body, being many, are one body: so also is Christ.

Manifestations of the Spirit of Divination:

Fortune-tellers or soothsayers:	Micah 5:12 and Isaiah 2:6
Warlocks, witches, or sorcerers:	Exodus 22:18
Stargazers, the zodiac, horoscopes:	Isaiah 47:13 and Leviticus 19:26
Rebellion:	1 Samuel 15:23
Hypnotists or enchanters:	Deuteronomy 18:11 and Isaiah 19:3
Drugs:	Galatians 5:20; and Revelation 9:1-2, 18:23, 21:8, and 22:15
Water-witching:	Hosea 4:12
Magic:	Exodus 7:11, 8:7, and 9:11

Roots—works of the flesh:

Romans 1:18-28, Galatians 5:19, Ephesians 5:8, and 1 Corinthians 6:9

PRAYER MODEL

Lord, in the name of Jesus, I thank You for Your Word that has made me aware of my sin. Forgive me for any past or current

involvement in occult activities. I love You, Jesus, and I want to live a life that is pleasing to You.

I bind Satan, in the name of Jesus, by the power and authority of the Word of God, I bind satan and the spirit of divination according to Matthew 18:18, which clearly states, "Whatsoever you shall bind on earth shall be bound in heaven." Any relationship built by me or my family with powers of darkness are now dissolved, in the name of Jesus.

Thank You, Lord, for freeing me. I worship You. According to Matthew 18:18, which promises, "Whatsoever ye shall loose on earth shall be loosed in heaven," I loose the power of the Holy Ghost in my life to restore and fill me with Your power. Give me a thirst for Your Word. Thank You, God for hearing and answering my prayer. Amen.

FAMILIAR SPIRIT

A familiar spirit and a spirit of divination are very similar.

Even though someone may have accepted Christ as his savior, it is still necessary to renounce in an audible voice any past experiences he or members of his family may have had with any of these practices. The ability to contact spirits is often passed from one generation to the next within receptive families, which may account for the name, "familiar." *Be filled with the Spirit of God* (Ephesians 5:18). This will keep you clear of demonic influences.

Xtreme Times POWER

BIND the Familiar Spirit

Matthew 18:18
[18] Verily I say unto you, Whatsoever ye shall bind on earth shall be bound in heaven: and whatsoever ye shall loose on earth shall be loosed in heaven.

LOOSE the Holy Spirit; Gifts of the Spirit

1 Corinthians 12:9-12
[9] To another faith by the same Spirit; to another the gifts of healing by the same Spirit;
[10] To another the working of miracles; to another prophecy; to another discerning of spirits; to another divers kinds of tongues; to another the interpretation of tongues:
[11] But all these worketh that one and the selfsame Spirit, dividing to every man severally as he will.
[12] For as the body is one, and hath many members, and all the members of that one body, being many, are one body: so also is Christ.

Manifestations of the Familiar Spirit:

Necromancers:	Deuteronomy 18:11 and Chronicles 10:13
Mediums:	1 Samuel 28
Clairvoyants:	1 Samuel 28:7-8
Spirits:	1 Samuel 28
Drugs or hallucinogens:	Revelation 9:21, 18:23, 21:8, and 22:15; and Galatians 5:20
Passive minds or dreamers:	Jeremiah 23:16, 25, 32; 27:9-10
Whispering and muttering:	Isaiah 8:19, 29:4, and 59:3
False prophecy:	Isaiah 8:19 and 29:4

BREAKING POWERS OF DARKNESS

Roots—works of the flesh:

Romans 1:18-28, Galatians 5:19, Ephesians 5:8, and 1 Corinthians 6:9

PRAYER MODEL

Lord, I thank You for Your Word that has made me aware of my sin. Forgive me for any past or current involvement in occult activities of satan. I confess my love to You, Jesus, and I want to live a life that is pleasing to You.

I bind satan in the name of Jesus. I bind the familiar spirit according to Matthew 18:18, which clearly states, "Whatsoever you shall bind on earth shall be bound in heaven." Any relationship between a familiar and me or my family is null and void from this point on.

Thank You, Lord, for freeing me. I worship You. According to Matthew 18:18, which promises, "Whatsoever ye shall loose on earth shall be loosed in heaven," I loose the power of the Holy Ghost in my life to restore and fill me with Your power. Give me a thirst for Your Word. Thank You, God, for hearing and answering my prayer. Amen.

THE WORD

Leviticus 19:31
31 Regard not them that have familiar spirits, neither seek after wizards, to be defiled by them: I am the LORD your God.

Xtreme Times POWER

Deuteronomy 18:10-11
[10] There shall not be found among you any one that maketh his son or his daughter to pass through the fire, or that useth divination, or an observer of times, or an enchanter, or a witch,
[11] Or a charmer, or a consulter with familiar spirits, or a wizard, or a necromancer.

Isaiah 8:19
[19] And when they shall say unto you, Seek unto them that have familiar spirits, and unto wizards that peep, and that mutter: should not a people seek unto their God? for the living to the dead?

Acts 16:16
[16] And it came to pass, as we went to prayer, a certain damsel possessed with a spirit of divination met us, which brought her masters much gain by soothsaying:

1 Corinthians 12:9-12
[9] To another faith by the same Spirit; to another the gifts of healing by the same Spirit;
[10] To another the working of miracles; to another prophecy; to another discerning of spirits; to another divers kinds of tongues; to another the interpretation of tongues:
[11] But all these worketh that one and the selfsame Spirit, dividing to every man severally as he will.
[12] For as the body is one, and hath many members, and all the members of that one body, being many, are one body: so also is Christ.

SPIRIT OF JEALOUSY

Jealousy and pride are probably the oldest sins in the universe. They are mentioned in Numbers 5:14. Lucifer let pride and jealousy corrupt him (Ezekiel 28:12-19).

BREAKING POWERS OF DARKNESS

Satan gained dominion over earth when Adam and Eve sinned, breaking the pure fellowship with God. Life then became a difficult battle against nature and the elements.

Twice, the Bible says that Cain was *"wroth and his countenance fell"* (Genesis 4:5, 6). People who do not control their anger open themselves up to the spirit of jealousy.

BIND the Spirit of Jealousy

Matthew 18:18
18 Verily I say unto you, Whatsoever ye shall bind on earth shall be bound in heaven: and whatsoever ye shall loose on earth shall be loosed in heaven.

LOOSE God's Love

1 John 4:16
16 And we have known and believed the love that God hath to us. God is love; and he that dwelleth in love dwelleth in God, and God in him.

Manifestations of the Spirit of Jealousy:

Murder:	Genesis 4:8
Revenge, spite, and grudges:	Proverbs 6:34; 14:16-17
Anger and rage:	Genesis 4:5-6; and Proverbs 6:34, 14:29, 22:24-25, and 29:22-23
Cruelty:	Song of Solomon 8:6 and Proverbs 27:4
Jealousy:	Numbers 5:14 and 30
Hate:	Genesis 37:3-8 and 1 Thessalonians 4:8
Causes and divisions:	Galatians 5:19
Extreme competiveness:	Genesis 4:4-5

Xtreme Times POWER

Strife: Proverbs 10:12
Contentiousness   Proverbs 13:10

Roots—works of the flesh:

Hatred, jealousy, divisiveness envy, lack of mercy, covetousness, causing debate and strife

PRAYER MODEL

I come in the name of Jesus, recognizing that I have left myself open to attacks of jealousy. Forgive me, and help me to live a life free of this and a life that is pleasing to You.

I bind satan and the spirit of jealousy in the name of Jesus, according to Matthew 18:18, which tells me, "Whatsoever ye shall bind on earth shall be bound in heaven." You no longer have an open door in my life through this spirit.

Thank You, Lord, for giving me freedom over the power of the devil. According to Matthew 18:18, which promises, "Whatsoever ye shall loose on earth shall be loosed in heaven," I loose the love of God in my life to flood my being so completely that I will "overcome evil with good." Help me to read Your Word faithfully each day. Thank You, Lord, for hearing and answering my prayer. Amen.

THE WORD

Psalm 27:10
[10] *When my father and my mother forsake me, then the LORD will take me up.*

BREAKING POWERS OF DARKNESS

Psalm 143:8
⁸ Cause me to hear thy loving kindness in the morning; for in thee do I trust: cause me to know the way wherein I should walk; for I lift up my soul unto thee.

Proverbs 27:4
⁴ Wrath is cruel, and anger is outrageous; but who is able to stand before envy?

Isaiah 48:17-18
¹⁷ Thus saith the LORD, thy Redeemer, the Holy One of Israel; I am the LORD thy God which teacheth thee to profit, which leadeth thee by the way that thou shouldest go.
¹⁸ O that thou hadst hearkened to my commandments! then had thy peace been as a river, and thy righteousness as the waves of the sea:

Matthew 6:25
²⁵ Therefore I say unto you, Take no thought for your life, what ye shall eat, or what ye shall drink; nor yet for your body, what ye shall put on. Is not the life more than meat, and the body than raiment?

Ephesians 5:2
² And walk in love, as Christ also hath loved us, and hath given himself for us an offering and a sacrifice to God for a sweetsmelling savour.

Galatians 6:4-5
⁴ But let every man prove his own work, and then shall he have rejoicing in himself alone, and not in another.
⁵ For every man shall bear his own burden.

Xtreme Times POWER

1 Thessalonians 4:9
⁹ But as touching brotherly love ye need not that I write unto you: for ye yourselves are taught of God to love one another.

SPIRIT OF LYING

God never changes; man changes, but God doesn't. This is important in the discussion of the lying spirit. God ALWAYS speaks the truth.

Satan is the father of all lies. He is the inventor of lying.

Not everyone who lies is possessed by a lying spirit. But each lie takes the person another step toward that condition.

Areas in which a lying spirit is involved are: superstitions, gossip, backbiting, false prophets and teachers, strong delusions, deceptions, and lies.

BIND the Spirit of Lying

Matthew 18:18
¹⁸ Verily I say unto you, Whatsoever ye shall bind on earth shall be bound in heaven: and whatsoever ye shall loose on earth shall be loosed in heaven.

LOOSE the Spirit of Truth

John 14:17
¹⁷ Even the Spirit of truth; whom the world cannot receive, because it seeth him not, neither knoweth him: but ye know him; for he dwelleth with you, and shall be in you.

BREAKING POWERS OF DARKNESS

Manifestations of the Spirit of Lying:

Strong deceptions:	2 Thessalonians 2:9-13
Flattery:	Psalm 78:36, and Proverbs 20:19 and 26:28
Superstitions:	1 Timothy 4:7
Accusations:	Revelation 12:10
False prophecy:	Jeremiah 23:15-17 and 27:9-10
Religious bondage:	Galatians 5:1
Slander:	Proverbs 10:18
Gossip:	1 Timothy 6:20 and 2 Timothy 2:16
Lies:	2 Chronicles 18:22 and Proverbs 6:16-19
False teachers:	2 Peter

Roots—works of the flesh:

Being untruthful, whispering, foolish talking, backbiting, breaking covenants, and extortion

PRAYER MODEL

I confess leaving myself open to attacks of a lying spirit and I ask forgiveness in the name of Jesus Christ. Help me, Lord, to put my faith and trust in You from this time forward!

I bind satan and the lying spirit in the name of Jesus, according to Matthew 18:18, which informs me, "Whatsoever ye shall bind on earth shall be bound in heaven." I close this open door to the lying spirit in my life in the name of Jesus.

Thank You, Lord, for giving me victory over the lying spirit. According to Matthew 18:18, which promises, "Whatsoever ye shall loose on earth shall be loosed in heaven," I loose the spirit

of truth in my life. Help me to read Your Word each day so that I can maintain the dominion over satan that I need in these last days. Thank You, Lord, for guiding my life and answering my prayer. Amen.

THE WORD

John 14:7
7 If ye had known me, ye should have known my Father also: and from henceforth ye know him, and have seen him.

John 14:26
26 But the Comforter, which is the Holy Ghost, whom the Father will send in my name, he shall teach you all things, and bring all things to your remembrance, whatsoever I have said unto you.

John 16:13
13 Howbeit when he, the Spirit of truth, is come, he will guide you into all truth: for he shall not speak of himself; but whatsoever he shall hear, that shall he speak: and he will shew you things to come.

Revelation 21:8
8 But the fearful, and unbelieving, and the abominable, and murderers, and whoremongers, and sorcerers, and idolaters, and all liars, shall have their part in the lake which burneth with fire and brimstone: which is the second death.

PERVERSE SPIRIT

Isaiah 19:14 *The LORD hath mingled a perverse spirit in the midst thereof: and they have caused Egypt to err in every work thereof, as a drunken man staggereth in his vomit.*

BREAKING POWERS OF DARKNESS

It may seem that this passage of scripture blames God for actions of this evil spirit. God does not need the help of perverse spirits to accomplish His will on earth, and that is evidenced in God's Word. The correct interpretation of this passage is that God took His hands off of a continual sin, allowing the perverse spirit to wreak havoc on Egypt.

When people insist on continuing to do the unnatural, God steps back and a reprobate mind develops. Once this happens, those people become twisted in their thinking, and they believe their lifestyle is normal.

This happens over time. It starts with small flirtations with wrong and expands into huge, perverted things that eventually takes over their lives.

BIND the Perverse Spirit

Matthew 18:18
18 Verily I say unto you, Whatsoever ye shall bind on earth shall be bound in heaven: and whatsoever ye shall loose on earth shall be loosed in heaven.

LOOSE the Excellent Spirit

Proverbs 17:27
27 He that hath knowledge spareth his words: and a man of understanding is of an excellent spirit.

Xtreme Times POWER

Manifestations of the Perverse Spirit:

Wounded spirits:	Proverbs 15:4
Evil actions:	Proverbs 17:20-23
Atheists:	Proverbs 14:2 and 19:3, Romans 1:30
Doctrinal errors:	Isaiah 19:14, Romans 1:22-23, 2 Timothy 3:10-11
Twisting the Word of God:	Acts 13:10 and 2 Peter 2:14
Contentiousness:	Phil. 2:14-16, 1 Timothy 6:4-5, and Titus 3:10-11
Chronic worrying:	Proverbs 19:2
Filthy minds:	Proverbs 2:12-15 and 22:33
Sexual perversions:	Proverbs 2:12-15; 22:33
Pornography:	Proverbs 2:12-15 and 22:33
Child abuse:	Romans 1:17-32 and 2 Timothy 3:2
Incest:	Romans 1:17-32 and 2 Timothy 3:2

Roots—works of the flesh:

Inventors of evil, heresies, sodomy, fornication, backbiting, ungodliness, and effeminate behavior

PRAYER MODEL

Lord, in the name of Jesus, forgive me for allowing a perverse spirit access to my life. I realize these actions not only place me in spiritual danger, but they also grieve You. I want to please You, Father, with all my heart.

Satan, in the name of Jesus, I bind your perverse spirit according to Matthew 18:18, which tells me, "Whatsoever ye shall bind

on earth shall be bound in heaven." You no longer have an open door in my life through this spirit.

Thank You, Lord, for giving me freedom over the power of the devil. According to Matthew 18:18, which promises, "Whatsoever ye shall loose on earth shall be loosed in heaven," I loose a good and excellent spirit, which is the Holy Spirit, to guide me in a life of purity. Help me to reprogram my mind on a daily basis by reading Your Word. Thank You, Lord, for confirming Your Word in my life. Amen.

THE WORD

Nehemiah 9:20
20 Thou gavest also thy good spirit to instruct them, and withheldest not thy manna from their mouth, and gavest them water for their thirst.

Daniel 5:12
12 Forasmuch as an excellent spirit, and knowledge, and understanding, interpreting of dreams, and shewing of hard sentences, and dissolving of doubts, were found in the same Daniel, whom the king named Belteshazzar: now let Daniel be called, and he will shew the interpretation.

1 Timothy 6:4
4 He is proud, knowing nothing, but doting about questions and strifes of words, whereof cometh envy, strife, railings, evil surmisings,

Proverbs 23:32-33
32 At the last it biteth like a serpent, and stingeth like an adder.
33 Thine eyes shall behold strange women, and thine heart shall utter perverse things.

SPIRIT OF HAUGHTINESS OR PRIDE

It is not possible to fall further than satan did. He fell from the most beautiful creation of God to the pit of hell.

The spirit of haughtiness keeps us from becoming the creation that God wants us to be, the best possible person that we can possibly be. We only realize that objective to the extent that we open ourselves to God.

When we are "I-centered," we open ourselves to this spirit of haughtiness.

BIND the Spirit of Haughtiness or Pride

Matthew 18:18
18 Verily I say unto you, Whatsoever ye shall bind on earth shall be bound in heaven: and whatsoever ye shall loose on earth shall be loosed in heaven.

LOOSE a Humble and Contrite Spirit

Isaiah 57:15
15 For thus saith the high and lofty One that inhabiteth eternity, whose name is Holy; I dwell in the high and holy place, with him also that is of a contrite and humble spirit, to revive the spirit of the humble, and to revive the heart of the contrite ones.

BREAKING POWERS OF DARKNESS

Manifestations of the Spirit of Haughtiness:

Pride:	Proverbs 16:16-17, 16:18-19, and 28:25; and Isaiah 16:6
Obstinacy:	Proverbs 29:1 and Daniel 5:20
Arrogance and smugness:	2 Samuel 22:28, Jeremiah 48:29, and Isaiah 2:11-17 and 5:15
Idleness:	Ezekiel 16:49-50
Rebelliousness:	1 Samuel 15:23 and Proverbs 29:1
Scornfulness:	Proverbs 1:22, 3:34, 21:24, and 29:8
Self-Righteousness:	Luke 18:11-12
Contentiousness:	Proverbs 13:10
Rejection of God:	Psalm 10:4 and Jeremiah 43:2
Self-deception:	Jeremiah 49:16

Proverbs 16:18
Pride goeth before destruction, and an haughty spirit before a fall.

Roots—works of the flesh:

Boastfulness, self-centeredness, presumptuousness, loftiness, self-exaltation, conceit, and arrogance

Isaiah 64:6
True humility is recognizing that, all our righteousness are as filthy rags; and that we can do nothing without the help and direction of God in our life.

We are in the world, but not of the world. All around us, and often very close to us, there are immoral and non-spiritual elements which, if allowed to penetrate our defenses, will surely "sink" us. Those elements must be kept out at all costs.

Xtreme Times POWER

PRAYER MODEL

Lord, in the name of Jesus, I see that I have not allowed You to reign supreme in my life. Forgive me for this terrible sin. I humbly bow before You with a contrite spirit and ask that You make something beautiful out of my life.

Satan, in the name of Jesus, I bind your haughty spirit according to Matthew 18:18, which tells me, "Whatsoever ye shall bind on earth shall be bound in heaven." I recognize you for what you are, a thief and a robber. I refuse to allow you to lead me away from God's will for my life.

Thank You, Lord, for Your forgiveness of this terrible sin. According to Matthew 18:18, which promises, "Whatsoever ye shall loose on earth shall be loosed in heaven," I loose a humble spirit, a spirit of holiness in my life to lead me in the path that You choose for me to walk. I recognize that I can find that path best by reading and studying Your Word, which, "is a lamp unto my feet, and a light unto my path" (Psalms 119:105) Thank You, Lord, for hearing and answering my prayer. Amen.

THE WORD

Proverbs 16:19
19 Better it is to be of an humble spirit with the lowly, than to divide the spoil with the proud.

Proverbs 21:4
4 An high look, and a proud heart, and the plowing of the wicked, is sin.

BREAKING POWERS OF DARKNESS

1 Thessalonians 2:6
⁶ Nor of men sought we glory, neither of you, nor yet of others, when we might have been burdensome, as the apostles of Christ.

James 4:6
⁶ But he giveth more grace. Wherefore he saith, God resisteth the proud, but giveth grace unto the humble.

1 Peter 5:5
⁵ Likewise, ye younger, submit yourselves unto the elder. Yea, all of you be subject one to another, and be clothed with humility: for God resisteth the proud, and giveth grace to the humble.

1 John 2:15-16
¹⁵ Love not the world, neither the things that are in the world. If any man love the world, the love of the Father is not in him.
¹⁶ For all that is in the world, the lust of the flesh, and the lust of the eyes, and the pride of life, is not of the Father, but is of the world.

SPIRIT OF HEAVINESS

Isaiah 61:3
To appoint unto them that mourn in Zion, to give unto them beauty for ashes, the oil of joy for mourning, the garment of praise for the spirit of heaviness; that they might be called trees of righteousness, the planting of the LORD, that he might be glorified.

It is natural to enter into a period of mourning after the loss of someone or something that we deeply value. We do not mourn indefinitely. Grief is a God-given emotion that allows us to empty out the deep feelings, but grief, if continued for a long period, can become neurotic, immature, and destructive. Isaiah 53:4

tells us that *"Surely he hath borne our griefs, carried our sorrows:"* We release them to God and go on with life. His grace is sufficient, and we must remember that excessive mourning is a trap with which the enemy would love to trip us in order to open doors of other strongholds.

BIND the Spirit of Heaviness

Matthew 18:18
18 Verily I say unto you, Whatsoever ye shall bind on earth shall be bound in heaven: and whatsoever ye shall loose on earth shall be loosed in heaven.

LOOSE the Comforter, Garment of Praise, and Oil of Joy

Psalm 45:7
7 Thou lovest righteousness, and hatest wickedness: therefore God, thy God, hath anointed thee with the oil of gladness above thy fellows.

Manifestations of the Spirit of Heaviness:

Excessive mourning:	Isaiah 6:13 and Luke 4:18
Sorrow and grief:	Nehemiah 2:2 and Proverbs 15:13
Insomnia:	Nehemiah 2:2
Self-pity:	Psalm 69:20
Despair, dejection, hopelessness:	2 Corinthians 1:8-9
Broken-heartedness	Psalm 69:20; Proverbs 12:18, 15:3, 13, and 18:14; and Luke 4:18
Depression:	Isaiah 61:3
Heaviness:	Isaiah 61:3

BREAKING POWERS OF DARKNESS

Suicidal Tendencies: Mark 9
Inner pain: Luke 4:18

Roots—works of the flesh:

Weakness, despondency, dullness, dark moods, failure, faintness, restraint, Gothic

PRAYER MODEL

God, I come to You in the name of Jesus. I don't really feel like praying. I'm doing it in obedience to Your Word. Forgive me for neglecting my time of prayer with You and the reading of Your Word. I've allowed the spirit of heaviness to rob me of the good things You have for me. But I promise to reject those thoughts of self-pity and to make praise to You a way of life from this time forth.

Satan, in the name of Jesus, I bind your spirit of heaviness according to Matthew 18:18, which promises, "Whatsoever ye shall bind on earth shall be bound in heaven." I recognize that you have taken advantage of me. Now I resist you in the name of Jesus. James 4:7 says, "Resist the devil, and he will flee from you." Go, in the name of Jesus, and don't bother coming back again.

Thank You, God, for delivering me from the trap of the enemy. According to Matthew 18:18, which says, "Whatsoever ye shall loose on earth shall be loosed in heaven," I loose the comforter, which is the Holy Spirit; the garment of praise, and the oil of joy. I praise Your holy name. Thank You, Jesus, for Your goodness and mercy to me. Thank You for hearing and answering my prayer. Amen.

Xtreme Times POWER

THE WORD

John 15:26
²⁶ But when the Comforter is come, whom I will send unto you from the Father, even the Spirit of truth, which proceedeth from the Father, he shall testify of me:

Romans 1:4
⁴ And declared to be the Son of God with power, according to the spirit of holiness, by the resurrection from the dead:

SPIRIT OF JEZEBEL

The Jezebel spirit seeks to hide itself, seduce, intimidate, manipulate, murder, and trade in human souls.

The Jezebel spirit worked powerfully through Queen Jezebel, a Sidonian princess who married King Ahab of Israel and killed many prophets of God. Jezebel also is mentioned in the book of Revelation, Chapter 2, verse 20, in the context of the church of Thyatira. Here, she is called a false prophetess, a teacher of sexual immorality. In this passage, a Jezebel is a person who comes under the influence of this spirit because the Lord says he gave her time to repent.

The Spirit of Jezebel/Mystery of Babylon/Harlot Spirit is a very religious spirit, but it promotes religious things that are contrary to God. Jezebel promotes fleshly indulgence among God's people and shuns the cross.

The Jezebel spirit is the enemy of true prophets of the Lord. The book of Revelation devotes a chapter to exposing this spirit

BREAKING POWERS OF DARKNESS

(Chapter 17). This chapter reveals a woman drunk with the blood of the saints and with the blood of the martyrs of Jesus (Revelation 17:6).

This spirit especially hates and seeks to murder righteous people and those who speak faithfully the Word of the Lord, just as Jezebel, the wife of Ahab, was responsible for most of the deaths of true prophets of Yahweh in her day (1 Kings 18:13).

This harlot spirit has an influence beyond that of the mystery of Babylon in influencing Christians to pollute their minds with Hollywood, pornography, sexual immorality, worldly pleasures, and the absence of godliness! Global political, economic, and religious systems now seek to unite all people under the Antichrist spirit. It has insinuated itself into the church, exercising godless control and seduction by having a form of godliness but denying the power! It seeks to kill the prophetic in apostolic ministry, neutralizing God's power!

Living a carnal life, wallowing in fleshly pleasure and fantasy while telling yourself that you are a Christian will allow you to operate under the spirit-of-Jezebel radar somewhat. But as long as it controls you, you are held captive. To say no to this spirit is to experience a tidal wave of opposition. Try to break free and you will experience the torment of attack. To continue to live in the sin of carnality is death (Luke 13:5). You have no choice but to break free!

God promises to judge and destroy this spirit and its works, but that doesn't come without pain of denying oneself!

Xtreme Times POWER

We see and experience the Jezebel spirit at work all around us. Its power grows as more people give themselves over to it, many of whom have no clue what they are doing.

We can win against this spirit! We do it by taking a rigid stand for truth in an age of religious expediency, convenience, and compromised Christian living.

Embracing the cross and nurturing one's relationship with Christ will break the chains of bondage, setting us free from the tentacles of an enemy that is out to kill, steal, and destroy.

More information on the effects of the spirit of Jezebel can be found in the book of Revelation. The effects are prevalent in religion, government, and individuals during the end time.

BIND the Spirit of Jezebel

Matthew 18:18
[18] Verily I say unto you, Whatsoever ye shall bind on earth shall be bound in heaven: and whatsoever ye shall loose on earth shall be loosed in heaven.

LOOSE the Spirit of Jehu

2 Kings 9:22
[22] And it came to pass, when Joram saw Jehu, that he said, Is it peace, Jehu? And he answered, What peace, so long as the whoredoms of thy mother Jezebel and her witchcrafts are so many?

BREAKING POWERS OF DARKNESS

Manifestations of the Spirit of Jezebel:

Silencing God's prophets:	1 Kings 18:4 and 1 Kings 19:1-3
Worship of idols:	1 Kings 16:31
Sexual immorality, orgies:	Isaiah 47 and Revelation 2:20
Being controlling:	1 Kings 21:5-15
Intimidation:	1 Kings 18
Fear:	1 Kings 18
Deception:	1 Kings 18

Roots—works of the flesh:

Self-pity, making accusations, indecision, aggression, intimidation, seeking attention, making insinuations, arrogance, insecurity, acting beguiling, feeling inadequate, belittling others, intellectualism, bickering, backbiting, interfering, brashness, bossiness, jealousy, envy, engaging in bedroom blackmail, acting like Jezebel, being conniving, lacking confidence, contentiousness, lying, continuous complaining, lawlessness, condemning others, laziness, confusion, manipulation, counterfeit spiritual gifts, mistrust, conditional love, nagging, charming, overindulgence, controlling spirits, pouting, dissatisfaction, pride, being demanding, perversion (sexual and spiritual), double mindedness, psychology, doubt, philosophy, disunity, projected guilt, discord, being quick-tempered, disruptiveness, retaliation, distrust, extracting revenge, deception, rationalization, delusion, rebellion, strife, defeat, slander, determined maneuvers, sharp temper, dominance, emotional outbursts, sorcery, failure, shirking responsibilities, fear, being sensitive, frustration, sharp tongue, forsaking protection, sleepiness, female dominance and control, shame, female hardness, suicide, fierce determination, spiritual blindness, false sickness, self-defeating attitudes, finger pointing, sorrow, frigidity, turmoil, grief, ungodly discipline, hatred of men, unbelief, ugliness, hasty marriages, vanity, hopelessness, witchcraft, hypnotic control, worldly wisdom, inability to give or receive love, whining, irresponsibility, seeking perfection, and obsessiveness, to name a few.

PRAYER MODEL

I come to You in the name of Jesus Christ, my savior and my redeemer. I thank You for showing me the error of my ways and allowing me the opportunity to repent. I know that You love me and that Your outstretched hands are reaching for me even as I speak. I come boldly to You, admitting my need for deliverance and healing that only You, through the Holy Spirit, can give.

I admit my wrong attitude toward the authority figures You have placed in my life. I confess that I have rebelled against Your Word through my behavior. Please, show me how my need to control and manipulate others came into my life that I may close the door to this forever. I choose now to forgive everyone who has ever hurt or abused me in any way. I do now forgive the following people by name (call them aloud). I confess that my lifestyle has been sinful and abusive, and ask Your forgiveness and cleansing. I humble myself before You and offer no excuses for my actions. Right now, in the name of Jesus, I renounce the evil work of all witchcraft control, domination, and manipulation, and I turn away from all such activity in my life.

I choose to break all ungodly ties with those I have sought to control, dominate, or manipulate. In the name of Jesus Christ, my Lord, I break the ungodly ties with and release the following people by name (those I have manipulated). By an act of my will,

BREAKING POWERS OF DARKNESS

I submit to all authority You have placed in my life. I trust my submission and obedience to Your Word to keep me, protect me, and bless me.

Open my eyes, Heavenly Father, to truly and clearly see Your Word and grant me the strength of will to walk in it. In the name of Jesus Christ and through the power of Your shed blood, I bind the strongman of Jezebel, and command it and all associated unclean spirits to leave me. I loose the spirit of Jehu, according to Matthew 18:18.

In the name of Jesus Christ, I command the following demonic spirits to leave me now; I repent and renounce participating with (name the spirits from the Roots list that have operated in your life) and ask for Your forgiveness.

THE WORD

1 Kings 16:31
31 And it came to pass, as if it had been a light thing for him to walk in the sins of Jeroboam the son of Nebat, that he took to wife Jezebel the daughter of Ethbaal king of the Zidonians, and went and served Baal, and worshipped him.

1 Kings 21:25
25 But there was none like unto Ahab, which did sell himself to work wickedness in the sight of the LORD, whom Jezebel his wife stirred up.

Romans 12:9
9 Let love be without dissimulation. Abhor that which is evil; cleave to that which is good.

Xtreme Times POWER

Revelation 2:20
[20] *Notwithstanding I have a few things against thee, because thou sufferest that woman Jezebel, which calleth herself a prophetess, to teach and to seduce my servants to commit fornication, and to eat things sacrificed unto idols.*

SPIRIT OF WHOREDOMS

The spirit of whoredom seems to imply that it is a spirit of prostitution, only. In reality, there is more to it than that.

This condition can be a spiritual bondage as well as physical one.

Hosea 4:12
My people ask counsel at their stocks, and their staff declareth unto them: for the spirit of whoredoms hath caused them to err, and they have gone a whoring from under their God.

Hosea 5:4
They will not frame their doings to turn unto their God: for the spirit of whoredoms is in the midst of them, and they have not known the LORD.

Although we may not offer sacrifices to a physical idol, whatever comes between us and our relationship with God is an idol and a form of spiritual adultery, though sex may not be involved.

Whatever rules us is our god. Food, diversions, sports, money, power, sex, pursuit of career, video games, television, Internet, a possession, hunting, fishing, our children, a religion, or a cause. It must not become between us and God.

BREAKING POWERS OF DARKNESS

BIND the Spirit of Whoredoms

Matthew 18:18
18 Verily I say unto you, Whatsoever ye shall bind on earth shall be bound in heaven: and whatsoever ye shall loose on earth shall be loosed in heaven.

LOOSE the Spirit of Truth

John 8:32
32 And ye shall know the truth, and the truth shall make you free.

Manifestations of the Spirit of Whoredoms:

Unfaithfulness:	Ezekiel 16:15, Proverbs 5:1-14
Spirit, soul, or body Prostitution:	Ezekiel 16:15, Proverbs 5:1-14
Love of money:	Proverbs 15:27, 1 Timothy 6:7-14
Self-Pity:	Psalm 69:20
Chronic dissatisfaction:	Ezekiel 16:28
Fornication:	Hosea 4:13-19
Idolatry:	Judges 2:17, Ezekiel 16, Hosea 4:12
Inordinate love of food:	1 Corinthians 6:13-16, Philippians 3:19
Worldliness:	James 4:4

Roots—works of the flesh:

Lust, harlotry, body exhibition, idolatry, seduction, love of the world, greed, and lust for power

Xtreme Times POWER

PRAYER MODEL

Father, I come to You in the name of Jesus. Forgive me for not keeping You first in my life. Forgive me for allowing the works of the flesh and the things of this world to creep in and displace You as the God of my life. I make You Lord of my life, now and forever more, and I promise to follow the instruction of Your Word.

Satan, in the name of Jesus, I bind your spirit of whoredoms according to Matthew 18:18, which promises, "Whatsoever ye shall bind on earth shall be bound in heaven." I refuse to allow your paltry imitations of deity to dominate my life. I denounce your idols and rebuke you in the name of Jesus.

Thank You, Father, for loosing me from the gods of this world. According to Matthew 18:18, which states, "Whatsoever ye shall loose on earth shall be loosed in heaven," I loose the spirit of God in my life. Help me to keep my priorities straight in these confusing days so I will be able to please You and accomplish Your will in my life. Thank You for hearing and answering my prayer. Amen.

THE WORD

Hosea 4:12
12 My people ask counsel at their stocks, and their staff declareth unto them: for the spirit of whoredoms hath caused them to err, and they have gone a whoring from under their God.

Hosea 5:4
4 They will not frame their doings to turn unto their God: for the spirit of whoredoms is in the midst of them, and they have not known the LORD.

BREAKING POWERS OF DARKNESS

Ephesians 3:16
16 That he would grant you, according to the riches of his glory, to be strengthened with might by his Spirit in the inner man;

SPIRIT OF SODOMY

(Homosexuality)

According to Genesis 19:4-5, before the two angels of the Lord retired for the night, the men of Sodom, young and old, surrounded the house and demanded that the two men be turned out to them so that they could have sex with them!

We are facing this aggressive spirit today in our world. It is a most deadly spirit; the quickest way to rouse the unquenchable anger and judgment of Almighty God is homosexuality. This spirit is wrapping its coils around the very throat of our world and unapologetically squeezing the moral life out of us. The proper word is sodomy, but even the terminology has been dressed up so as to sound less brutish.

Throughout the Bible, two spirits are met with disgust and destruction from God, murder and homosexuality. In history, we see two direct instances of God's total destruction of cities that were overrun with homosexuality. Sodom and Gomorrah were so annihilated that nothing remains but the Dead Sea. Pompeii was drowned in a sea of hot, molten lava because of the great stench of perversion that arose from the city in 79 AD.

This spirit manipulates individuals aggressively to demand laws that force acceptance of this unthinkable wickedness. John 7:24 tells us to judge with righteous judgment and 1 Thessalonians

Xtreme Times POWER

5:22-28 tells us to abstain from all appearance of evil! Leviticus 18:22-23 calls homosexuality an abomination, and says that it was so despicable under the law that individuals caught in the act were to be put to death!

This is not a spirit that can be left alone or ignored. It is like a cancer that spreads when it is ignored. We must oppose sodomy (homosexuality) and speak out against it. Our children must understand that it is not an acceptable alternative lifestyle. We should not hate sodomites but should firmly oppose their sin, as the Word of God commands us.

BIND the Spirit of Sodomy

Matthew 18:18
[18] Verily I say unto you, Whatsoever ye shall bind on earth shall be bound in heaven: and whatsoever ye shall loose on earth shall be loosed in heaven.

LOOSE the Spirit of Truth

Romans 10:9-11
[9] That if thou shalt confess with thy mouth the Lord Jesus, and shalt believe in thine heart that God hath raised him from the dead, thou shalt be saved.
[10] For with the heart man believeth unto righteousness; and with the mouth confession is made unto salvation.
[11] For the scripture saith, Whosoever believeth on him shall not be ashamed.

BREAKING POWERS OF DARKNESS

Manifestations of the Spirit of Sodomy:

Sexual aggression:	Genesis 19:1-11
Unnatural lust:	Romans 1
Malicious behavior:	Romans 1:18-32
Idol worship:	1 Corinthians 6:9-11
Ungodliness:	1 Timothy 1:8-10
Sexual perversion:	Jude 7
Fornication:	1 Corinthians 6:9
Works of the flesh:	Galatians 5:19
Uncleanness:	Ephesians 5:3-7, Colossians 3:5-7
Sin justification:	Titus 1:16

Roots—works of the flesh:

Lust, sodomy, perversion, abusing another, defilement, and unnatural affection

PRAYER MODEL

Father, I come to You in the name of Jesus. Forgive me for allowing perverseness in my life. Forgive me for allowing works of the flesh and unnatural wickedness in my life.

In the name of Jesus and by the power and authority of Jesus Christ, I bind the spirit of sodomy. According to Matthew 18:18, "Whatsoever ye bind on earth shall be bound in heaven." I refuse to let this abominable lifestyle and spirit to have dominion over me any longer and take authority of it in Jesus's name!

Thank You, Jesus, for loosening me from the god of this world. According to Matthew 18:18, "Whatsoever ye loose on earth shall

be loosed in heaven." I loose the spirit of truth to reign in my life. Please strengthen my resolve and commitment to be like Christ and I pray for His will to be completed in my life.

THE WORD

Genesis 2:24
[24] Therefore shall a man leave his father and his mother, and shall cleave unto his wife: and they shall be one flesh.

Genesis 13:13
[13] But the men of Sodom were wicked and sinners before the LORD exceedingly.

Genesis 18:20
[20] And the LORD said, Because the cry of Sodom and Gomorrah is great, and because their sin is very grievous;

Genesis 19:4-5 (NIV)
[4] Before they had gone to bed, all the men from every part of the city of Sodomboth young and old–surrounded the house.
[5] They called to Lot, "Where are the men who came to you tonight? Bring them out to us so that we can have sex with them."

Leviticus 18:21-22
[21] And thou shalt not let any of thy seed pass through the fire to Molech, neither shalt thou profane the name of thy God: I am the LORD.
[22] Thou shalt not lie with mankind, as with womankind: it is abomination.

Hosea 4:12
[12] My people ask counsel at their stocks, and their staff declareth unto them: for the spirit of whoredoms hath caused them to err, and they have gone a whoring from under their God.

BREAKING POWERS OF DARKNESS

Matthew 19:5-6
⁵ And said, For this cause shall a man leave father and mother, and shall cleave to his wife: and they twain shall be one flesh?
⁶ Wherefore they are no more twain, but one flesh. What therefore God hath joined together, let not man put asunder.

John 7:24
²⁴ Judge not according to the appearance, but judge righteous judgment.

1 Thessalonians 5:22
²² Abstain from all appearance of evil.

SPIRIT OF INFIRMITY

Luke 13:11-13
¹¹ And, behold, there was a woman which had a spirit of infirmity eighteen years, and was bowed together, and could in no wise lift up herself.
¹² And when Jesus saw her, he called her to him, and said unto her, Woman, thou art loosed from thine infirmity.
¹³ And he laid his hands on her: and immediately she was made straight, and glorified God.

Luke was careful to explain that the spirit of infirmity uses sickness to bind people, making those infirmities the work of satan. As believers, we receive by faith the promises of God in His Word, which include divine healing.

Mark 11:24
²⁴ Therefore I say unto you, What things soever ye desire, when ye pray, believe that ye receive them, and ye shall have them.

Xtreme Times POWER

When you pray, believe that you will receive it!

BIND the Spirit of Infirmity

Matthew 18:18
[18] Verily I say unto you, Whatsoever ye shall bind on earth shall be bound in heaven: and whatsoever ye shall loose on earth shall be loosed in heaven.

LOOSE the Spirit of Life, Gifts of Healing

1 Corinthians 12:9
[9] To another faith by the same Spirit; to another the gifts of healing by the same Spirit

Manifestations of the Spirit of Infirmity:

Bent body or spine:	Luke 13:11
Impotence, frailty, lameness:	John 5:5, Acts 3:2 and 4:9
Weakness:	Luke 13:11, John 5:5
Lingering disorders:	Luke 13:11, John 5:5
Cancer:	Luke 13:11, John 5:5
Oppression:	Acts 10:38

Roots—works of the flesh:

Feebleness, frailty, and weakness

PRAYER MODEL

Father, in the name of Jesus, I come to You boldly as You have instructed me to do in Hebrews 4:16. I thank You for Your healing

power that is as strong today as it has ever been. I receive Your healing right now by faith in Your Word. I believe that if You took my infirmities and bore my sicknesses, then by Your stripes *I am healed!*

In the name of Jesus, I bind the spirit of infirmity according to Matthew 18:18, which says "Whatsoever ye bind on earth shall be bound in heaven." I demand in the name of Jesus that you leave me alone and never return to harass me again.

Thank You, Jesus, for healing me, and I loose the spirit of life into every cell of my body according to Matthew 18:18, which promises, "Whatsoever ye shall loose on earth shall be loosed in heaven." I promise to listen to Your Word so my faith will be strong and grow. I shall continually praise You for healing me from this day on. Amen.

THE WORD

Romans 8:2
² For the law of the Spirit of life in Christ Jesus hath made me free from the law of sin and death.

1 Corinthians 12:9
⁹ To another faith by the same Spirit; to another the gifts of healing by the same Spirit.

DUMB AND DEAF SPIRIT

Mark 9:17-29
¹⁷ And one of the multitude answered and said, Master, I have brought unto thee my son, which hath a dumb spirit. The rest of this passage

of scripture describes the son and various things concerning this spirit, and Jesus's rebuking of the spirit and casting it out.

Evil spirits make people do off-the-wall things because satan is basically dumb. *Satan thought* that he was capable of dethroning God, which shows his IQ. This doesn't mean that he is incapable of making life miserable for us and we can drop our defenses. Satan still has vast knowledge of human nature that he uses to his advantage. But we should not give him more credit than he deserves.

Analyze the things that people do under the influence of satan. They do weird things. If people are dressed, they want to take their clothes off. If quiet is appropriate, they are loud; and vice versa. What is smart about a person sucking smoke out of a white cylinder and getting lung cancer? What is intelligent about someone drinking—or worse, forcing chemicals into their veins—and then getting into a vehicle and killing innocent people? It happens 25,000 times every year in the United States alone.

Our Authority: Mark 16:17-18
[17] And these signs shall follow them that believe; In my name shall they cast out devils; they shall speak with new tongues;
[18] They shall take up serpents; and if they drink any deadly thing, it shall not hurt them; they shall lay hands on the sick, and they shall recover.

We must live close to the Lord at all times to hear and know the voice of God. If our body is dominating us so that we cannot hear the voice of the spirit when He speaks to us, then we need to discipline our body by fasting so that it will learn to be quiet when God speaks. Our prayer life must be current at all times!

BREAKING POWERS OF DARKNESS

BIND the Dumb and Deaf Spirit

Matthew 18:18
18 Verily I say unto you, Whatsoever ye shall bind on earth shall be bound in heaven: and whatsoever ye shall loose on earth shall be loosed in heaven.

LOOSE the Resurrection, Life, and Healing

Philippians 3:10
10 That I may know him, and the power of his resurrection, and the fellowship of his sufferings, being made conformable unto his death.

Manifestations of the Dumb and Deaf Spirit

Dumbness:	Mark 9:25
Crying:	Mark 9:18, 20, and 26
Mental illness:	Matthew 17:15, Mark 9:17, and Mark 5:5
Foaming at the mouth:	Luke 9:39, Mark 9:20
Seizures/epilepsy:	Mark 9:18, 20, and 26
Suicide, drowning, burning:	Mark 9:22
Excessive crying:	Mark 9:26
Pining away:	Mark 9:18
Blindness:	Mark 12:22
Prostration:	Mark 9:26
Ear problems:	Mark 9:25, 26

Roots—works of the flesh:

Dumbness, deafness, speechlessness, lamenting, mourning

Xtreme Times POWER

PRAYER MODEL

Satan, in the name of Jesus, I bind your dumb and deaf spirit according to Matthew 18:18, which tells me, "Whatsoever ye shall bind on earth shall be bound in heaven." I demand that you stop harassing me this instant. Leave me and never return, you foul spirit!

Thank You, Jesus, for giving me freedom from all of the forces of the enemy. I loose Your Holy Spirit in my life according to Matthew 18:18, which states, "Whatsoever ye shall loose on earth shall be loosed in heaven." I loose Resurrection, life, and the gifts of healing to do a complete job in my body and soul. And I appropriate Your victory over satan in every area of my life. Amen.

THE WORD

Mark 9:25
^{25} When Jesus saw that the people came running together, he rebuked the foul spirit, saying unto him, Thou dumb and deaf spirit, I charge thee, come out of him, and enter no more into him.

Romans 8:11
^{11} But if the Spirit of him that raised up Jesus from the dead dwell in you, he that raised up Christ from the dead shall also quicken your mortal bodies by his Spirit that dwelleth in you.

1 Corinthians 12:9
^{9} To another faith by the same Spirit; to another the gifts of healing by the same Spirit.

BREAKING POWERS OF DARKNESS

SPIRIT OF BONDAGE

Romans 8:15
For ye have not received the spirit of bondage again to fear; but ye have received the Spirit of adoption, whereby we cry, Abba, Father.

There is nothing like returning home at the end of a day's work and having your son or daughter run to you and jump into your arms, crying, "Daddy, Daddy." It doesn't matter who you are or what type of position you have in society; to your child, you are plain "Daddy." That is the type of relationship that God longs to have with his creation; the creation to whom he gave *choice*. When we long to commune with him, talk with him, worship him, or mimic Him as a child would copy his mom or dad, that is the kind of relationship God wants to have with us. He wants to be a loving father, gathering us to him and loving us with an everlasting love.

Bondage is a horrible thing. A person bound by vices of evil is sad. Worse is seeing someone who was once bound in the mire of satan but had been freed by the blood of Christ choose to crawl back into the pit and throw himself onto the heap for more punishment. It is unbelievable that after tasting the freedom of God, one would return to satan's bondage. Sadly, however, it happens. It happens because *total* bondage doesn't occur in one day. It is a gradual process of compromising here and saying OK there to satisfy the flesh. Before he realizes it, the individual is back to wallowing in the sin over which he once had victory.

We must follow the Word, not our feelings. Whether we feel confident or not, the Word is the authority of God and is ours!

Xtreme Times POWER

BIND the Spirit of Bondage

Matthew 18:18
¹⁸ Verily I say unto you, Whatsoever ye shall bind on earth shall be bound in heaven: and whatsoever ye shall loose on earth shall be loosed in heaven.

LOOSE the Liberty and Spirit of Adoption

Romans 8:15
¹⁵ For ye have not received the spirit of bondage again to fear; but ye have received the Spirit of adoption, whereby we cry, Abba, Father.

Manifestations of the Spirit of Bondage:

Fears:	Romans 8:15
Addictions:	Romans 8:15, 2 Peter 2:19
Fear of death:	Hebrews 2:14, 15
Captivity to satan:	2 Peter 2:19
Bondage to sin:	2 Timothy 2:26
Being a servant of corruption:	Romans 7:23, Luke 8:26-29
Compulsive sinning:	Proverbs 5:22, John 8:34

Roots—works of the flesh:

Slavery, servitude to sin

PRAYER MODEL

Dear Father, I come to You realizing that only You can free me from the web of satan. Thank You for Your great love for me. I desire to call You "Abba Father" and feel Your arms of love

wrapped around me so I won't have to seek love from a bottle or any of the other false hopes that satan has dangled before my eyes. Satan promises so much and delivers so little. Forgive me for my sins, and I promise to serve You the rest of my life.

Satan, I rebuke you in the name of Jesus and bind your spirit of bondage according to Matthew 18:18, which states, "Whatsoever ye shall bind on earth shall be bound in heaven." I see you now as you really are—a spiritual "spider" trying to bind and paralyze me with cords of habits and bondage. In the name of Jesus, I command you to leave me alone and never return.

Thank You, Lord, for Your beautiful freedom. I loose the spirit of adoption in my life according to Matthew 18:18, which promises, "Whatsoever ye shall loose on earth shall be loosed in heaven." Help me to continue on forever in the freedom of Your Holy Spirit. I promise to read Your Word and walk by faith, not by sight or feelings, so that I can obey Your will for my life. Amen.

THE WORD

Romans 8:15
15 For ye have not received the spirit of bondage again to fear; but ye have received the Spirit of adoption, whereby we cry, Abba, Father.

Romans 8:23
23 And not only they, but ourselves also, which have the firstfruits of the Spirit, even we ourselves groan within ourselves, waiting for the adoption, to wit, the redemption of our body.

Galatians 2:4
⁴ And that because of false brethren unawares brought in, who came in privily to spy out our liberty which we have in Christ Jesus, that they might bring us into bondage:

2 Timothy 1:7
⁷ For God hath not given us the spirit of fear; but of power, and of love, and of a sound mind.

Hebrews 2:15
¹⁵ And deliver them who through fear of death were all their lifetime subject to bondage.

SPIRIT OF FEAR

There are two types of fear: positive and negative.

Positive fear is a natural protection that keeps us from hurting ourselves. We don't grab a blazing piece of wood or stand in water and put our fingers in an electrical socket. We can characterize this fear as a "deep respect." We "respect" fire or electricity and God, so we obey the laws. *The fear of the LORD is the beginning of wisdom* (Psalm 111:10). I obey God's commandments because I respect Him for who He is.

Negative fear chokes out faith, joy, peace, and love. It binds, paralyzes, and weakens Christians and softens them up for the arrival of other spirits, such as infirmity and bondage. Medical science tells us that fear can cause many kinds of sickness. In reality, negative fear is the negative "faith" of the devil. We believe satan more than God's word when we allow fear to reign in our lives. Fear is directly opposed to God's laws. For this reason, *"But the fearful, and unbelieving, and the abominable, and murderers, and whoremongers, and sorcerers, and idolaters, and all liars, shall have their part in the lake which burneth with fire and brimstone: which is the second death* (Revelation 21:8).

WARNING! Natural positive fear can escalate to the point that a spirit of fear takes over if the individual isn't careful to understand what's going on. For example, an accident or trauma can cause natural fear to expand into negative fear, inspired and magnified by the spirit of fear.

1 Timothy 4:1. *Now the Spirit speaketh expressly, that in the latter times some shall depart from the faith, giving heed to seducing spirits, and doctrines of devils.*

BIND the Spirit of Fear

Matthew 18:18
[18] Verily I say unto you, Whatsoever ye shall bind on earth shall be bound in heaven: and whatsoever ye shall loose on earth shall be loosed in heaven.

LOOSE Love, Power, and Sound Mind

2 Timothy 1:7
[7] For God hath not given us the spirit of fear; but of power, and of love, and of a sound mind.

Xtreme Times POWER

Manifestations of the Spirit of Fear:

Fears, phobias:	Isaiah 13:7, 2 Timothy 1:7
Heart attacks:	Psalms 55:4, Luke 21:26, and John 14:1 and 14:27
Fear of death:	Psalms 55:4, Hebrews 2:14 and 15
Nightmares, terrors:	Psalms 91:5
Anxiety, stress:	1 Peter 5:7
Lack of trust, doubt:	Matthew 8:26, Revelation 21:8
Fear of man:	Proverbs 29:15

Roots—works of the flesh:

Timidness, faithlessness, and fearfulness

PRAYER MODEL

Father, I see that fear is not from You. I understand that fear, worry, and doubt are the negative faith of the enemy. Forgive me for ever doubting Your ability to watch over and care for me. I will trust You from this time forth as my source of security.

Satan, in the name of Jesus, I bind your spirit of fear according to Matthew 18:18, which says very clearly, "Whatsoever ye bind on earth shall be bound in heaven." I will not stand for your attacks of fear. Leave me alone this very instant and never return. If you try, I'll use the Sword of the Spirit against you.

Thank You, Lord, for Your peace, power, love and sound mind. I loose Your Holy Spirit in my life according to Matthew 18:18, which promises, "Whatsoever ye shall loose on earth shall be loosed in heaven." I refuse to allow fear to rob me of all the

good things You have for Your children. I claim the mind of Christ from this day forward. Thank You for delivering me from fear. Amen.

THE WORD

Psalm 46:1-3
¹ God is our refuge and strength, a very present help in trouble.
² Therefore will not we fear, though the earth be removed, and though the mountains be carried into the midst of the sea;
³ Though the waters thereof roar and be troubled, though the mountains shake with the swelling thereof. Selah.

Psalm 56:3-4
³ What time I am afraid, I will trust in thee.
⁴ In God I will praise his word, in God I have put my trust; I will not fear what flesh can do unto me.

John 14:27
²⁷ Peace I leave with you, my peace I give unto you: not as the world giveth, give I unto you. Let not your heart be troubled, neither let it be afraid.

Romans 8:15
¹⁵ For ye have not received the spirit of bondage again to fear; but ye have received the Spirit of adoption, whereby we cry, Abba, Father.

SEDUCING SPIRIT

1 Timothy 4:1. *Now the Spirit speaketh expressly, that in the latter times some shall depart from the faith, giving heed to seducing spirits, and doctrines of devils.*

Xtreme Times POWER

Seducing spirits will be especially active in the latter days of time as evilness becomes nearly irresistible. Their prime targets will be people who bear the name of Jesus and who are washed in the blood of the lamb, and baptized in the name of Jesus Christ for the remission of their sins. This is the group that will be targeted by satan, playing both ends against the middle. If he can't entice the born-again Christian with the usual sins, he uses false religion to trap them. For a variety of reasons, these blood-bought, blood-washed believers will leave God's truth and embrace religions invented by devils.

Many religions have popped up and gained momentum as we watch this unfold, including the church of satan, where every abominable thing imaginable takes place.

How does satan seduce a Christian?

James 1:14-15
14 But every man is tempted, when he is drawn away of his own lust, and enticed.
15 Then when lust hath conceived, it bringeth forth sin: and sin, when it is finished, bringeth forth death.

BIND the Seducing Spirit

Matthew 18:18
18 Verily I say unto you, Whatsoever ye shall bind on earth shall be bound in heaven: and whatsoever ye shall loose on earth shall be loosed in heaven.

BREAKING POWERS OF DARKNESS

LOOSE the Holy Spirit and Truth

John 16:13
¹³ Howbeit when he, the Spirit of truth, is come, he will guide you into all truth: for he shall not speak of himself; but whatsoever he shall hear, that shall he speak: and he will shew you things to come.

Manifestations of the Seducing Spirit:

Hypocritical lies:	1 Timothy 4:1
Seared conscience:	1 Timothy 4:1
Attractions (fascination with false prophets, signs, wonders, etc.):	Mark 13:22
Deceit:	2 Timothy 3:13, 1 John 2:18-26
Fascination with evil objects or persons:	Proverbs 12:26
Wandering from the truth:	2 Timothy 3:13, 1 John 2:18-26
Being seduced or enticed:	1 Timothy 4:1, 2 Timothy 3:13

Roots—works of the flesh:

Deceit, seduction, being an imposter, misleading

PRAYER MODEL

Father, forgive me for allowing the world to creep into my heart and life. I can see how deceptive the enemy is and I know only Your Word can guide me through the spiritual minefields that lie ahead. I promise to read Your Word each day and seek Your guidance for my life.

Xtreme Times POWER

Satan, in the name of Jesus, I bind your seducing spirits according to Matthew 18:18, which says, "Whatsoever ye bind on earth, shall be bound in heaven." I realize you are trying to cause me to depart from the faith, so I command you to leave me alone from this moment on. I have chosen to follow. You have no part of me, satan. Leave in the name of Jesus.

Thank You, Jesus, for freeing me from the evil spirits that were trying to deceive me. I loose Your Holy Spirit in my life according to Matthew 18:18, which tells me, "Whatsoever ye shall loose on earth shall be loosed in heaven." I thank You for giving me the victory over every power of the enemy, and I appropriate the mind of Christ to be mine according to Your promises. Amen.

THE WORD

1 John 4:1-3
¹ Beloved, believe not every spirit, but try the spirits whether they are of God: because many false prophets are gone out into the world.
² Hereby know ye the Spirit of God: Every spirit that confesseth that Jesus Christ is come in the flesh is of God:
³ And every spirit that confesseth not that Jesus Christ is come in the flesh is not of God: and this is that spirit of antichrist, whereof ye have heard that it should come; and even now already is it in the world.

1 John 4:4-6
⁴ Ye are of God, little children, and have overcome them: because greater is he that is in you, than he that is in the world.
⁵ They are of the world: therefore speak they of the world, and the world heareth them.
⁶ We are of God: he that knoweth God heareth us; he that is not of God heareth not us. Hereby know we the spirit of truth, and the spirit of error.

BREAKING POWERS OF DARKNESS

2 Corinthians 11:3
³ But I fear, lest by any means, as the serpent beguiled Eve through his subtilty, so your minds should be corrupted from the simplicity that is in Christ.

SPIRIT OF ANTICHRIST

According to *Strong's Concordance,* Greek word number 473, "Antichrist," means "instead of Christ."

1 John 4:3
And every spirit that confesseth not that Jesus Christ is come in the flesh is not of God: and this is that spirit of antichrist, whereof ye have heard that it should come; and even now already is it in the world.

The **spirit of Antichrist** attacks the very foundation of Christianity: the virgin birth of Jesus Christ. If Jesus was not God in the flesh then all of His other claims, such as the Atonement, Healing, the Baptism of the Holy Ghost, the Resurrection of the dead, the Rapture of the Church, and the Lord's second coming, are all false.

The **spirit of Antichrist** works through those who teach that Jesus was a good man but nothing more.

Through different religions, our schools and colleges, the government, and various organizations, world opinion is being shaped to accept satan's counterfeit for Christ. The world blindly accepts satan's latest programs as the greatest things ever proposed, never questioning evil, but always questioning good. People are plunging recklessly toward the abyss of hopelessness, taken in by the snares of evil. They are no match for satan as they succumb to the lust of their own flesh and wallow in self-righteousness. Meanwhile, satan screams in laughter as another one is snared.

We are to judge their words by the Word of God and then mark them as being from this world's system, under the command of satan, and send them packing.

2 John 1
[10] If there come any unto you, and bring not this doctrine, receive him not into your house, neither bid him God speed:
[11] For he that biddeth him God speed is partaker of his evil deeds.

BIND the Spirit of Antichrist

Matthew 18:18
[18] Verily I say unto you, Whatsoever ye shall bind on earth shall be bound in heaven: and whatsoever ye shall loose on earth shall be loosed in heaven.

LOOSE the Spirit of Truth

1 John 4:6
[6] We are of God: he that knoweth God heareth us; he that is not of God heareth not us. Hereby know we the spirit of truth, and the spirit of error.

Manifestations of the Spirit of Antichrist:

Denial of the deity of Christ:	1 John 4:3, 2 John 7
Denial of atonement:	1 John 4:3
Opposing Christ's teaching:	2 Thessalonians 2:4, 1 John 4:3
Humanism:	2 Thessalonians 2:3, 7
Worldly speech and actions:	1 John 4:5

BREAKING POWERS OF DARKNESS

Opposing Christians: Revelation 13:7
Deceivers: 2 Thessalonians 2:4, 2 John 7
Lawlessness: 2 Thessalonians 2:3-12

Roots—works of the flesh:

Contrast, requital, instead, and substitution of Christ

PRAYER MODEL

Lord, thank You for Your Word and spirit that will guide me through the last, evil days of this age. I place my trust completely in You. Your Word states without doubt that, "Heaven and earth shall pass away: but my words shall not pass away." Thank You for that promise. Forgive me for ever doubting Your ability to take care of me.

Satan, in the name of Jesus, I rebuke your spirit of Antichrist. I will not be dominated by your evil strongman, because greater is He that is in me than he that is in the world. I am an overcomer in the name of Jesus. I bind your spirit of Antichrist according to Matthew 18:18, which promises, "Whatsoever ye shall bind on earth shall be bound in heaven." You cannot operate in my life because the Greater One dwells within me.

Thank You, God, for showing me the Way, the Truth, and the Life. I can relax in You because You have provided for my every need as I cooperate with You, Your Word, and Your Holy Spirit. I loose Your Holy Spirit in my life according to Matthew 18:18, which says, "Whatsoever ye shall loose on earth shall be loosed in heaven." Thank You, Lord, for walking with me until the end of this age.

Xtreme Times POWER

THE WORD

John 17:12
¹² While I was with them in the world, I kept them in thy name: those that thou gavest me I have kept, and none of them is lost, but the son of perdition; that the scripture might be fulfilled.

2 Thessalonians 2:10
¹⁰ And with all deceivableness of unrighteousness in them that perish; because they received not the love of the truth, that they might be saved.

2 Thessalonians 2:12
¹² That they all might be damned who believed not the truth, but had pleasure in unrighteousness.

2 John 1:7
⁷ For many deceivers are entered into the world, who confess not that Jesus Christ is come in the flesh. This is a deceiver and an antichrist.

SPIRIT OF ERROR

1 John 4
We are of God: he that knoweth God heareth us; he that is not of God heareth not us. Hereby know we the spirit of truth, and the spirit of error.

The **spirit of error** works best when there is ignorance of God's Word. No one deliberately sets out to believe a false religion. People are deceived into it because it *appears* to be the truth. Our world is filled with mirages urging lost souls to follow them to truth they so desperately need. But a relentless foe leads lost souls through a terrain of deceptiveness, turning their worlds into horror stories of blindness, unless they have a map to guide them. Jesus cries out to these beat-up wrecks of humanity, *"If any man thirst, let him come unto me, and drink"* (John 7:37).

Minds are clouded by the spirit of error to the degree that an individual is absolutely convinced that he is right.

Patience is of the utmost importance when dealing with this spirit. We have to rely on the Holy Ghost to turn the light on and give the Word of God in small doses so that it doesn't overwhelm the individual and make him defensive.

BIND the Spirit of Error

Matthew 18:18
18 Verily I say unto you, Whatsoever ye shall bind on earth shall be bound in heaven: and whatsoever ye shall loose on earth shall be loosed in heaven.

LOOSE the Spirit of Truth

John 16:13
13 Howbeit when he, the Spirit of truth, is come, he will guide you into all truth: for he shall not speak of himself; but whatsoever he shall hear, that shall he speak: and he will shew you things to come.

Manifestations of the Spirit of Error:

Error:	Proverbs 14:22, 1 John 4:6, and 2 Peter 3:16 and 17
Refusing to be submissive:	Proverbs 29:1
False doctrines:	1 Timothy 6:20 and 21, 2 Timothy 4:3, Titus 3:10, and 1 John 4:1-6

Xtreme Times POWER

Being unteachable:	Proverbs 10:17, 12:1, 13:18, 15:10, 12, and 32; 2 Timothy 4:1-4; and John 4:6
Being a servant of corruption:	2 Peter 2:19
Being defensive or argumentative:	2 Peter 2
Contentiousness:	James 3:16
New Age Philosophy:	2 Thessalonians, 2 Peter 2:10

Roots—works of the flesh:

Having a reprobate mind, deceit, foolishness, profanity, unrighteousness, uncleanliness, having a form of Godliness

PRAYER MODEL

God, thank You for giving me a firm foundation to build my life upon. In this world so full of lies and deception, I can rest upon the truth of Your Word. Forgive me for trusting in myself. I place my life completely in Your hands. Forgive me for all of my sins. You are the Lord and savior of my life, and I promise to live according to Your Word from this moment on.

Satan, I bind your spirit of error in the name of Jesus according to Matthew 18:18, which promises, "Whatsoever ye shall bind on earth shall be bound in heaven." I refuse to follow your twisted ways and thoughts. I command you to leave, now, in the name of Jesus.

Thank You, Jesus. I love You with all my heart and I desire to serve You with all that is within me. I loose Your Holy Spirit of truth in

my life according to Matthew 18:18, which says, "Whatsoever ye shall loose on earth shall be loosed in heaven." I thank You for helping me to be more than a conqueror.

THE WORD

Psalms 51:10
¹⁰ Create in me a clean heart, O God; and renew a right spirit within me.

John 8:44
⁴⁴ Ye are of your father the devil, and the lusts of your father ye will do. He was a murderer from the beginning, and abode not in the truth, because there is no truth in him. When he speaketh a lie, he speaketh of his own: for he is a liar, and the father of it.

John 14:6
⁶ Jesus saith unto him, I am the way, the truth, and the life: no man cometh unto the Father, but by me.

SPIRIT OF DEATH

The spirit of death is not mentioned specifically by name in the Bible, but there are several reasons to believe that death is more than a condition or term.

Revelation 20:14 tells us that *"death and hell were cast into the lake of fire. This is the second death."* This is the second death of which John is not speaking symbolically. It is a place that actually exists. It seems that in this passage of scripture "death" has more meaning than a mere definition of the end of life of our flesh.

Xtreme Times POWER

In 1 Corinthians 15:26, Paul tells us that the last enemy that shall be destroyed is death.

Satan tries to impact all areas of a Christian's life with death. If he can't literally take your life, then expect him to try and kill your finances, marriage, friendships, family relationships, etc. The spirit of death is not just about death to life; it's about attacking you in any area that it possibly can.

1 Corinthians 15:26
²⁶The last enemy that shall be destroyed is death.

Revelation 20:10
¹⁰And the devil that deceived them was cast into the lake of fire and brimstone, where the beast and the false prophet are, and shall be tormented day and night for ever and ever.

Revelation 20:11
¹¹And I saw a great white throne, and him that sat on it, from whose face the earth and the heaven fled away; and there was found no place for them.

Revelation 20:14
¹⁴ And death and hell were cast into the lake of fire. This is the second death.

Paul says the last enemy to be destroyed is death, the devil is cast into the lake of fire, there is the great white throne of judgment, and then death is cast into the lake of fire.

A distinction definitely is made between the devil and death in these passages. Death, of course, is under the direction of satan.

BREAKING POWERS OF DARKNESS

But according to this description, it would seem that death is some kind of "being"—possibly a powerful fallen angel.

We must understand that God has the power over death, hell, and the grave, and he has given us the authority over the enemy through His righteousness, which is now *our* righteousness, since we took it on when we were buried in a watery grave of baptism in the name of Jesus Christ. That means we can shout along with Paul: *O death, where is thy sting? O grave, where is thy victory?* (1 Corinthians 15:55.)

BIND the Spirit of Death

Matthew 18:18
[18] Verily I say unto you, Whatsoever ye shall bind on earth shall be bound in heaven: and whatsoever ye shall loose on earth shall be loosed in heaven.

LOOSE the Spirit of Life

Romans 8:2
[2] For the law of the Spirit of life in Christ Jesus hath made me free from the law of sin and death.

PRAYER MODEL

God, my choice is Life to reign in my spirit, soul, and body from this day forward.

In the name of Jesus, I rebuke you, satan, and the spirit of death. Your attempts to destroy me are in vain because you have already

been condemned to the lake of fire. I refuse your robbery and devastation. Leave in the name of Jesus. You are under my feet!

Jesus, thank You for Your spirit of life that dwells within me and blesses everything that I attempt to do. I have the authority to bind and loose according to Matthew 18:18, which says, "Whatsoever ye shall loose on earth shall be loosed in heaven." I loose Your spirit of life to flow through me and overcome satan and his attacks.

THE WORD

Proverbs 10:2
² Treasures of wickedness profit nothing: but righteousness delivereth from death.

Proverbs 18:21
²¹ Death and life are in the power of the tongue: and they that love it shall eat the fruit thereof.

1 Corinthians 15:55
⁵⁵ O death, where is thy sting? O grave, where is thy victory?

1 John 14:6
⁶ Jesus saith unto him, I am the way, the truth, and the life: no man cometh unto the Father, but by me.

8

GOD

GOD

ONLY ONE GOD

There are over fifty passages of scripture that teach that God is one and that there is no other. The very meaning of the term "God" signifies the supreme, almighty one. There can be but one ultimate, all-inclusive God.
- Deuteronomy 4:35 tells us that *Jehovah is God, there is none else besides him!*
- Isaiah 44:6 says, *I am the first, and I am the last; and besides me there is no God.*
- Isaiah 43:10 says, *Before me there was no God formed, neither shall there be after me.*
- Isaiah 46:9 says, *For I am God, and there is none else; I am God, and there is none like me.*
- 1 Timothy 1:17 says, *Now unto the King eternal, immortal, invisible, the only God, (be) honor and glory forever and ever. Amen.*

Although God is omniscient, there is one thing that He does not know: He does not know another God.

GOD IS A SPIRIT

God is a spirit and as such, He has no physical limitations. He may be seen only in Jesus Christ. It is only as He is spirit that He can be omnipresent, everywhere at the same time, filling the universe. The Samaritan women asked, "Where is God to be found? On Mount Zion or Mount Gerizim?" To this question, Jesus answered that God is not confined to any one place. God is everywhere; the heaven and heaven of heavens cannot contain Him. This can only be if God is a spirit.
- Psalm 139:7: *Whither shall I go from thy Spirit? Or whither shall I flee from thy presence?*

- Jeremiah 23:24: *Can any hide himself in secret places so that I shall not see him? saith Jehovah. Do not I fill heaven and earth? saith Jehovah.*
- Colossians 1:15 and 1 Timothy 1:17: *God is a Spirit. He is invisible.*
- John 1:18: *No man has seen God at any time.*

Since God is a spirit, He must be worshipped in spirit and truth. This can be accomplished best with spirit-filled people having the revelation of the oneness truth, the Mighty God in Christ Jesus.

GOD WAS MANIFEST IN THE FLESH

In the incarnation, the Word became flesh, and in that flesh, the Mighty God was manifest.

INCARNATION: The dictionary definition of incarnation is "to embody in flesh."

In the incarnation, *the Word became flesh* (John 1:14) and *God was manifest in the flesh* (1 Timothy 3:16). This is correct Scriptural terminology. The Word was God; in the incarnation the Word became what He was not—flesh. Yet He became this without ceasing to be what He eternally was—God. God could not be born of Mary, but He did manifest Himself in that flesh that was born of Mary. The flesh that was born was the Word incarnate. This does not make two persons, for the Word was God. The one true God, who is a spirit, was the Father of the flesh that was born and, at the same time, manifested Himself in that flesh.

GOD

THE MIGHTY GOD IN CHRIST JESUS: The scripture states that *God was in Christ, reconciling the world unto himself* (2 Corinthians 5:19). Once we understand the truth expressed in this scripture, the revelation of the oneness of the Godhead becomes clear. We see Jesus Christ as both God and man, God manifesting Himself in flesh, and God in that human temple, reconciling the world to himself. Are there two persons who are reconciling us to themselves? No. *All things are of God, who hath reconciled us to HIMSELF by Jesus Christ* (2 Corinthians 5:18, emphasis added.) The scripture tells us that the only place we can find the Father is in Jesus Christ and the only place we can find the Son and the Holy Ghost is in Jesus Christ.

JESUS CHRIST WAS BOTH GOD AND MAN

In the incarnation, Jesus Christ possessed a dual nature: divinity and humanity. It should be clearly understood that Jesus was not two persons, nor did He possess two personalities. He was God-man, the Word incarnate, God manifest in flesh. As a human being, He was the Son; as God, He was the Father. As the Son, many times He spoke and acted as a man; as the Father, He spoke and acted as God.

Jesus was God and a perfect man. We do not use the word "perfect" with the Deity, for there are no degrees of perfection with God, but there are degrees of perfection with man. In His humanity, Jesus Christ was the Son of God. Sonship denotes a beginning; also a relation to time and place. Only as He became a man was He able to become the *only begotten Son* (John 3:16). He was not an eternal son or a created son, but a son who was conceived in the womb of Mary. As a son, He grew and matured and was subject to the Father. As a son, He tasted of our infirmities and weaknesses and was tempted in every point.

The purposes of the sonship were:
1. That He might become our redeemer. The necessity of the atonement demanded that there be a sinless sacrifice offered in our stead. Only God could provide such a sacrifice (Hebrews 2:14).
2. That He might become our mediator. Our mediator knows our weaknesses through His omniscience, and by way of actual experience (Hebrews 4:15).
3. That He might become our king. In order to have a kingdom there must be a king. He reigns now in our hearts, but soon He shall come to reign upon this earth (Matthew 26:64).
4. That He might be our judge (Acts 17:31).

ATTRIBUTES OF JESUS CHRIST

1. **OMNIPOTENCE:** Jesus said that "all power" was given unto Him. He is the almighty. Jesus revealed His omnipotence over disease, death, nature, and demons.
2. **OMNISCIENCE:** Jesus knew what was in man (John 2:24 and 25); of Him it was said that He knew all things (John 16:30). In Him are hidden *all* the treasures of wisdom and knowledge.
3. **OMNIPRESENCE:** God is everywhere. All things have their being in Him, but He is distinct from all things; He fills the universe, but is not mingled with it. He is the intelligence that guides and the power that moves; but His personality is preserved, and He is independent of the works of His hands, however vast and noble. Study Psalms 139, Hebrews 1:3, and Acts 17:27 and 28.

GOD

JESUS IS THE NAME OF THE FATHER, SON, AND HOLY GHOST

The prophet stated that there is *one Lord and His name one* (Zachariah 14:9). If we believe that there are three persons or three Gods, then we must have three names. A person is identified by his name. The prophet states his name is "One." In the Great Commission, as stated in Matthew 28:16 - 20, the scripture states to go into all the world baptizing in the name of the father, son, and Holy Ghost, which are titles. The name of the father, son and Holy Ghost is Jesus, the name is singular! Acts 4:12, tells us there is no other name given among men whereby we can be saved.

There are many titles of our God, all of which depict His offices and characteristics. Among them are the titles Father, Son, and Holy Ghost. In like manner, a man is body, soul, and spirit, but this is not the man's name. Would the bank cash a check that carries the signature, "Body, soul, and spirit"? The check must carry his signature, which is his name.

The testimony of scripture is overwhelming. It clearly states the truth and leaves no room for a shadow of doubt that the NAME OF DEITY IS JESUS.

There is no other name under heaven whereby we must be saved (Acts 4:12). Jesus is the SAVING NAME of our God. It is evident that Matthew 28:19 is being obeyed only when a person is baptized in the NAME OF JESUS. Whatever we do in word or deed, we must do in the name of Jesus (Colossians 3:17).

Xtreme Times POWER

THE WORD

Deuteronomy 6:4
4 Hear, O Israel: The LORD our God is one LORD:

1 Kings 8:27
27 But will God indeed dwell on the earth? behold, the heaven and heaven of heavens cannot contain thee; how much less this house that I have builded?

Isaiah 44:8
8 Fear ye not, neither be afraid: have not I told thee from that time, and have declared it? ye are even my witnesses. Is there a God beside me? yea, there is no God; I know not any.

Matthew 15:25
25 Then came she and worshipped him, saying, Lord, help me.

Matthew 18:20
20 For where two or three are gathered together in my name, there am I in the midst of them.

Luke 7:48
48 And he said unto her, Thy sins are forgiven.

Luke 24:39
39 Behold my hands and my feet, that it is I myself: handle me, and see; for a spirit hath not flesh and bones, as ye see me have.

John 1:3
3 All things were made by him; and without him was not any thing made that was made.

GOD

John 1:14
[14] And the Word was made flesh, and dwelt among us, (and we beheld his glory, the glory as of the only begotten of the Father,) full of grace and truth.

John 1:18
[18] No man hath seen God at any time; the only begotten Son, which is in the bosom of the Father, he hath declared him.

John 4:24
[24] God is a Spirit: and they that worship him must worship him in spirit and in truth.

John 5:43
[43] I am come in my Father's name, and ye receive me not: if another shall come in his own name, him ye will receive.

John 17:26
[26] And I have declared unto them thy name, and will declare it: that the love wherewith thou hast loved me may be in them, and I in them.

Acts 9:5
[5] And he said, Who art thou, Lord? And the Lord said, I am Jesus whom thou persecutest: it is hard for thee to kick against the pricks.

2 Corinthians 5:19
[19] To wit, that God was in Christ, reconciling the world unto himself, not imputing their trespasses unto them; and hath committed unto us the word of reconciliation.

Xtreme Times POWER

Philippians 2:8
⁸ And being found in fashion as a man, he humbled himself, and became obedient unto death, even the death of the cross.

Philippians 2:9
⁹ Wherefore God also hath highly exalted him, and given him a name which is above every name:

Colossians 2:3
³ In whom are hid all the treasures of wisdom and knowledge.

Colossians 2:9
⁹ For in him dwelleth all the fullness of the Godhead bodily.

1 Timothy 1:17
¹⁷ Now unto the King eternal, immortal, invisible, the only wise God, be honor and glory for ever and ever. Amen.

1 Timothy 2:5
⁵ For there is one God, and one mediator between God and men, the man Christ Jesus;

1 Timothy 3:16
¹⁶ And without controversy great is the mystery of godliness: God was manifest in the flesh, justified in the Spirit, seen of angels, preached unto the Gentiles, believed on in the world, received up into glory.

James 2:19
¹⁹ Thou believest that there is one God; thou doest well: the devils also believe, and tremble.

9

BAPTISM

BAPTISM

WATER BAPTISM

Water baptism is a basic requirement to a Christian's salvation. A series of questions usually arise in Water Baptism: "What is the Biblical way of doing it?" Is baptism performed by sprinkling? Or is it by immersion in water? Is it using the TITLES of Father, Son and Holy Ghost (Matt. 28:19), or using the NAME of the Lord Jesus Christ? (Acts 2:38)?

The Bible cannot contradict itself for it is the Word of God. It is imperative that we understand clearly what the bible says about this subject so that we follow biblical instruction..

There are two distinct meanings, washing and burial.

Washing

Matthew 3:5-6
5 Then went out to him Jerusalem, and all Judea, and all the region round about Jordan.
6 And were baptized of him in Jordan, confessing their sins.

Burial

Romans 6:4
4 Therefore we are buried with him by baptism into death: that like as Christ was raised up from the dead by the glory of the Father, even so we also should walk in newness of life.

Colossians 2:12
12 Buried with him in baptism, wherein also ye are risen with him through the faith of the operation of God, who hath raised him from the dead.

Xtreme Times POWER

FULFILLMENT OF THE COMMAND IN THE EARLY CHURCH

Acts 2:38
[38] Then Peter said unto them, Repent, and be baptized every one of you in the name of Jesus Christ for the remission of sins, and ye shall receive the gift of the Holy Ghost.

Acts 10:48
[48] And he commanded them to be baptized in the name of the Lord. Then prayed they him to tarry certain days.

Acts 19:5
[5] When they heard this, they were baptized in the name of the Lord Jesus.

Early Church Baptism

The word baptism comes from the Greek word *baptizo*, meaning to dunk, immerse, or soak.

John 3:23
[23] And John also was baptizing in Aenon near to Salim, because there was much water there: and they came, and were baptized.

Matthew 3:16
[16] And Jesus, when he was baptized, went up straightway out of the water: and, lo, the heavens were opened unto him, and he saw the Spirit of God descending like a dove, and lighting upon him:

Acts 8:38-39
[38] And he commanded the chariot to stand still: and they went down both into the water, both Philip and the eunuch; and he baptized him.

BAPTISM

[39] And when they were come up out of the water, the Spirit of the Lord caught away Philip, that the eunuch saw him no more: and he went on his way rejoicing.

Sprinkling

Sprinkling is not found in the scripture. Sprinkling, pouring, or infant baptism cannot be found or substantiated in the Word of God. These are only traditions.

The Baptism Formula Used

The birth of the church in the second chapter of Acts made John's baptism obsolete. It was updated when The Name was added to it.

Acts 2:38
[38] Then Peter said unto them, Repent, and be baptized every one of you in the name of Jesus Christ for the remission of sins, and ye shall receive the gift of the Holy Ghost.

The greatest legacy the Lord left his bride (the church) was His name!

Acts 4:12
[12] Neither is there salvation in any other: for there is none other name under heaven given among men, whereby we must be saved.

No Other Baptism Practiced in Scripture

Jesus's name must be invoked verbally to have a proper baptism!

Xtreme Times POWER

Acts 8:16
16 (For as yet he was fallen upon none of them: only they were baptized in the name of the Lord Jesus.)

Acts 10:48
48 And he commanded them to be baptized in the name of the Lord. Then prayed they him to tarry certain days.

Acts 19:5
5 When they heard this, they were baptized in the name of the Lord Jesus.

Romans 6:3
3 Know ye not, that so many of us as were baptized into Jesus Christ were baptized into his death?

Three Questions Paul Asked the Church at Corinth

1 Corinthians 1:13
13 Is Christ divided? Was Paul crucified for you? Or were ye baptized in the name of Paul?

Jesus was crucified for us, so we should be baptized in Jesus's name!

Look at Paul's own baptism:

Acts 22:16
16 And now why tarriest thou? arise, and be baptized, and wash away thy sins, calling on the name of the Lord.

BAPTISM

BAPTISM IS ESSENTIAL TO SALVATION

Acts 10:48
48 And he commanded them to be baptized in the name of the Lord. Then prayed they him to tarry certain days.

Mark 16:15-16
15 And he said unto them, Go ye into all the world, and preach the gospel to every creature.
16 He that believeth and is baptized shall be saved; but he that believeth not shall be damned.

Galatians 3:27
27 For as many of you as have been baptized into Christ have put on Christ.

Acts 2:41
41 Then they that gladly received his word were baptized: and the same day there were added unto them about three thousand souls.

Ephesians 4:5
5 One Lord, one faith, one baptism,

IS MATTHEW 28:19 A CONTRADICTION?

Matthew 28:19
19 Go ye therefore, and teach all nations, baptizing them in the name of the Father, and of the Son, and of the Holy Ghost:

Matthew 28:19 was obeyed in Acts 2:38. Father, Son, and Holy Ghost are titles, not names. Many repeat the Lord's command found in Matthew 28:19 instead of obeying it. Using a threefold formula for baptism was not practiced or taught by the disciples of Jesus Christ.

The Name of the Father

John 5:43
⁴³ I am come in my Father's name, and ye receive me not: if another shall come in his own name, him ye will receive.

The Name of the Son

John 20:31
³¹ But these are written, that ye might believe that Jesus is the Christ, the Son of God; and that believing ye might have life through his name.

The Name of the Holy Ghost

John 14:26:
²⁶ But the Comforter, which is the Holy Ghost, whom the Father will send in my name, he shall teach you all things, and bring all things to your remembrance, whatsoever I have said unto you.

The Holy Ghost is not a name; it is a title for **the spirit of God.**

One of the greatest revelations in the Bible: The message of who Jesus is!

10

WORD MADE FLESH

WORD MADE FLESH

John 1:14
[14] And the Word was made flesh, and dwelt among us, (and we beheld his glory, the glory as of the only begotten of the Father,) full of grace and truth.

THE MESSAGE

Sometimes the hearer listens to this passage, and hears the echoes from the Old Testament.

In the beginning

Long before modern science existed, the ancients knew that the universe had a beginning. Not a universe going through endless cycles of reincarnation, but a time in which time started, a place at which all places were defined. The issue seems so scientific now, but it was a leap of faith for the ancients; they saw a universe designed by a creator that was eternal, living in infinity, influenced only by His own creativity.

The universe is not eternal, because it's creator is eternal. The creator and the creation are not made equally or simultaneously. The universe is in time. Whoever created it therefore cannot be – or He would be part of the universe. And if He were part of the universe, how could He have caused His own creation? No, the eternal God solves the great problems of metaphysics!

Echoing the words of Genesis, "In the beginning" Genesis 1:1, means that God spoken of here – the Word - is one with God who was revealed to the ancients of Israel. There is no cosmic god proclaiming some pantheistic nonsense from the East. It is the stern Jehovah of Moses, Joshua, of Elijah and Isaiah, the God of Abraham, Isaac, and Jacob!

Indeed, there is more in this introduction. To echo the words of Genesis, "In the beginning" means that the God spoken of here – the Word – is one with the God who was revealed to ancient Israel. This is no cosmic god proclaiming some pantheistic nonsense from the East. It is the stern Jehovah of Moses and Joshua, of Elijah and Isaiah.

In the beginning was the Word

"The Word" is the way, the truth, and the life, John 14:6 and no one comes to the Father except by Him.

He is the "Word"-the Greek Strong's Number 3056 is logos - meaning that He is everything of the mind of God which is now revealed. A universal force of reason which governed the universe, creating all things by Logos.

"Was"the Word when time began, Christ was! He is Alpha, Omega, Beginning and End, Who Was and Is to come!

With God, and was God

"Hear O Israel: the Lord your God is one." Through time, He always was, will always be, and is God alone! He is the eternal immortal God!

The eternal God, who created all things chose not send us just a message, but The Message – in the person of The Messenger!

WORD MADE FLESH

The name of the Father, Son, and Holy Ghost is Jesus! The disciples never had a single conflict over baptism in the New Testament. Why? Because they understood the singleness or oneness of God.

John 14:8-11

⁸ Philip saith unto him, Lord, shew us the Father, and it sufficeth us.

⁹ Jesus saith unto him, Have I been so long time with you, and yet hast thou not known me, Philip? he that hath seen me hath seen the Father; and how sayest thou then, Shew us the Father?

¹⁰ Believest thou not that I am in the Father, and the Father in me? the words that I speak unto you I speak not of myself: but the Father that dwelleth in me, he doeth the works.

¹¹ Believe me that I am in the Father, and the Father in me: or else believe me for the very works' sake.

John 14:15-20

¹⁵ If ye love me, keep my commandments.

¹⁶ And I will pray the Father, and he shall give you another Comforter, that he may abide with you for ever;

¹⁷ Even the Spirit of truth; whom the world cannot receive, because it seeth him not, neither knoweth him: but ye know him; for he dwelleth with you, and shall be in you.

¹⁸ I will not leave you comfortless: I will come to you.

¹⁹ Yet a little while, and the world seeth me no more; but ye see me: because I live, ye shall live also.

²⁰ At that day ye shall know that I am in my Father, and ye in me, and I in you.

John 14:25-27

²⁵ These things have I spoken unto you, being yet present with you.

Xtreme Times POWER

26 But the Comforter, which is the Holy Ghost, whom the Father will send in my name, he shall teach you all things, and bring all things to your remembrance, whatsoever I have said unto you.
27 Peace I leave with you, my peace I give unto you: not as the world giveth, give I unto you. Let not your heart be troubled, neither let it be afraid.

Jesus said, *"I will not leave you comfortless, I will come to you."* THE HOLY GHOST IS JESUS IN SPIRIT FORM!

These three titles refer to the different roles of the same **One God!** He is Father in creation; Son in redemption; Holy Ghost in His body, the church!

2 Corinthians 5:19
19 To wit, that God was in Christ, reconciling the world unto himself, not imputing their trespasses unto them; and hath committed unto us the word of reconciliation.

Deuteronomy 6:4
4 Hear, O Israel: The LORD our God is one LORD:

Isaiah 9:6
6 For unto us a child is born, unto us a son is given: and the government shall be upon his shoulder: and his name shall be called Wonderful, Counselor, The Mighty God, The everlasting Father, The Prince of Peace.

11

END TIME POWER

ACTS 2:1-41

END TIME POWER

Acts 1:8
⁸ But ye shall receive power, after that the Holy Ghost is come upon you: and ye shall be witnesses unto me both in Jerusalem, and in all Judaea, and in Samaria, and unto the uttermost part of the earth.

The power of the Holy Ghost is essential in this end time hour to stand against the wiles of satan countering the spirit of Antichrist. We need all the power available to us, Acts 1:8 tells us we will receive power after that the Holy Ghost has come upon us.

HOLY GHOST POWER

Old Testament Prophecy

Ezekiel 36:26
²⁶ A new heart also will I give you, and a new spirit will I put within you: and I will take away the stony heart out of your flesh, and I will give you an heart of flesh.
²⁷ And I will put my spirit within you, and cause you to walk in my statutes, and ye shall keep my judgments, and do them.

Joel 2:28
²⁸ And it shall come to pass afterward, that I will pour out my spirit upon all flesh; and your sons and your daughters shall prophesy, your old men shall dream dreams, your young men shall see visions:

Jesus Prophesied It

John 7:38-39
³⁸ He that believeth on me, as the scripture hath said, out of his belly shall flow rivers of living water.

Xtreme Times POWER

³⁹ (But this spake he of the Spirit, which they that believe on him should receive: for the Holy Ghost was not yet given; because that Jesus was not yet glorified.)

Then It Happened

In the upper room on the Day of Pentecost, the Holy Ghost came upon the 120 gathered and they were all filled with the Holy Ghost!

Acts 2:1-4
¹ And when the day of Pentecost was fully come, they were all with one accord in one place.
² And suddenly there came a sound from heaven as of a rushing mighty wind, and it filled all the house where they were sitting.
³ And there appeared unto them cloven tongues like as of fire, and it sat upon each of them.
⁴ And they were all filled with the Holy Ghost, and began to speak with other tongues, as the Spirit gave them utterance.

You do not receive the Holy Ghost *automatically* when you believe! It is a separate but dynamic experience that is part of the new birth!

Acts 19:1-6
¹ And it came to pass, that, while Apollos was at Corinth, Paul having passed through the upper coasts came to Ephesus: and finding certain disciples,
² He said unto them, Have ye received the Holy Ghost since ye believed? And they said unto him, We have not so much as heard whether there be any Holy Ghost.

END TIME POWER

³ And he said unto them, Unto what then were ye baptized? And they said, Unto John's baptism.
⁴ Then said Paul, John verily baptized with the baptism of repentance, saying unto the people, that they should believe on him which should come after him, that is, on Christ Jesus.
⁵ When they heard this, they were baptized in the name of the Lord Jesus.
⁶ And when Paul had laid his hands upon them, the Holy Ghost came on them; and they spake with tongues, and prophesied.

Paul found believers, but they needed their *experience* with God *updated!* Even though they had been baptized unto John's baptism, it was not enough. They were baptized again in the name of the Lord Jesus.

The baptism of the Holy Ghost is a birth of the spirit in the experience of the believer. As breath enters the lungs of the newborn babe and he cries out, so does the Holy Ghost enter the heart of the newborn child of God and he speaks with tongues.

The following facts will help us understand the place of baptism of the Holy Ghost in God's plan of salvation:
1. Jesus never left it to the choice of His disciples; He *commanded* them to tarry until they received.
2. Jesus revealed how important it was for the comforter to come when He said that it was expedient for Him to go away (John 16:7).
3. The Apostle Peter was given the keys to the kingdom, and when he preached the gospel unlocking the door to the kingdom, he preached (a) repentance, (b) water baptism in Jesus's name, and (c) the baptism of the Holy Ghost. (John 3:5).

4. The Apostle Paul wrote that we are saved "by the washing of regeneration, and renewing of the Holy Ghost (Titus 3:5).

WE MUST BE BORN AGAIN

We must be born of water and spirit.

Jesus told Nicodemus, *Verily, verily, I say unto thee, Except a man be born again, he cannot see the kingdom of God* (John 3:3).

Nicodemus asked how? I'm an old man, how am I going to be born again?

Jesus answered, *That which is born of the flesh is flesh; and that which is born of the Spirit is spirit* (John 3:6).

Nicodemus said, *Except a man be born of water and of the Spirit, he cannot enter into the kingdom of God.* (John 3:5).

Not by works of righteousness which we have done, but according to his mercy he saved us, by the washing of regeneration, and renewing of the Holy Ghost (Titus 3:5).

Jesus said, *I am the way, the truth, and the life: no man cometh unto the Father, but by me* (John 14:6).

At that day ye shall know that I am in my Father, and ye in me, and I in you (John 14:20).

In Galatians 3:27, Paul wrote, *For as many of you as have been baptized into Christ have put on Christ.*

So how does he get in *you*? He gets in you through the *baptism* of the Holy Ghost. It takes the *baptism* of the water in the name of Jesus and the baptism of the Holy Ghost. It takes both of these to put you back into God; back into the kingdom; back into the abiding with God.

SPEAKING IN TONGUES

John 3:8
8The wind bloweth where it listeth, and thou hearest the sound thereof, but canst not tell whence it cometh, and whither it goeth: so is every one that is born of the Spirit.

The Bible shows us in many different ways that speaking in other tongues is the evidence of the infilling of the Holy Ghost.

Everyone who is born of the spirit is like the wind; you can't see it, but you can hear it!

Thou hearest what? **Sound!**

The original Greek word for sound is *fo-nay'*, which means noise, voice, or sound.

Replace the word "sound" with "fo-nay'" or "language" and you have: *The wind bloweth where it listeth, and thou hearest the LANGUAGE thereof.* And, the last verse: *so is every one that is born of the Spirit.*

Xtreme Times POWER

THE PROMISE

Acts 2:37-41
[37] Now when they heard this, they were pricked in their heart, and said unto Peter and to the rest of the apostles, Men and brethren, what shall we do?
[38] Then Peter said unto them, Repent, and be baptized every one of you in the name of Jesus Christ for the remission of sins, and ye shall receive the gift of the Holy Ghost.
[39] For the promise is unto you, and to your children, and to all that are afar off, even as many as the Lord our God shall call.
[40] And with many other words did he testify and exhort, saying, Save yourselves from this untoward generation.
[41] Then they that gladly received his word were baptized: and the same day there were added unto them about three thousand souls.

It is not God's will that any perish but all have everlasting life (2 Peter 3:9). All are called but few are chosen because few answer the call!

Not only is the infilling of the Holy Ghost God's salvation plan, we are endued with power when we receive the Holy Ghost (Acts 1:8). We need every bit of power available during this end time hour!

To Order:

THINGS TO COME — UNDERSTANDING THE END TIME www.thingstocome.cc

keith@keithfletcher.cc

ABOUT THE AUTHOR

Keith W. Fletcher resides in Northwest Louisiana, an international evangelist travelling and speaking extensively throughout the United States, as well as other countries throughout the world. God has blessed him to experience many people saved, delivered, and set free from the clutches of satan's end-time attack against humanity. He has witnessed many healings and miracles, and he has experienced mighty powerful moves of God! God has blessed this ministry and he gives God all the glory!

THINGS TO COME UNDERSTANDING THE END TIME www.thingstocome.cc

keith@keithfletcher.cc